Illusions of I

Illusions of Immortality

A Psychology of Fame and Celebrity

David Giles

First published in Great Britain 2000 by
MACMILLAN PRESS LTD
Houndmills, Basingstoke, Hampshire RG21 6XS and London
Companies and representatives throughout the world

A catalogue record for this book is available from the British Library.

ISBN 0-333-75449-2 hardcover
ISBN 0-333-75450-6 paperback

 First published in the United States of America 2000 by
ST. MARTIN'S PRESS, INC.,
Scholarly and Reference Division,
175 Fifth Avenue, New York, N.Y. 10010

ISBN 0-312-22943-7

Library of Congress Cataloging-in-Publication Data
Giles, David, 1964–
Illusions of immortality : a psychology of fame and celebrity / David Giles.
p. cm.
Includes bibliographical references and index.
ISBN 0-312-22943-7 (hardcover)
1. Fame. 2. Celebrities—Psychology. 3. Fame—Psychological aspects. I. Title.

BJ1470.5.G55 1999
306.4 21—dc21

99-042133

© David Giles 2000

All rights reserved. No reproduction, copy or transmission of this publication may be made without written permission.

No paragraph of this publication may be reproduced, copied or transmitted save with written permission or in accordance with the provisions of the Copyright, Designs and Patents Act 1988, or under the terms of any licence permitting limited copying issued by the Copyright Licensing Agency, 90 Tottenham Court Road, London W1P 0LP.

Any person who does any unauthorised act in relation to this publication may be liable to criminal prosecution and civil claims for damages.

The author has asserted his right to be identified as the author of this work in accordance with the Copyright, Designs and Patents Act 1988.

This book is printed on paper suitable for recycling and made from fully managed and sustained forest sources.

10   9   8   7   6   5   4   3   2   1
09   08   07   06   05   04   03   02   01   00

Printed in Hong Kong

Contents

List of Tables	viii

1 Introduction: defining fame and celebrity — 1
Fame and celebrity: definitions — 3
Fame as a process — 4
Special people — 6
Overview of the book — 9

2 'Mad for noblesse': fame through history — 12
The birth of Western civilization — 13
The origins of fame — 14
Fame through art and literature — 16
The dandy and the fraud — 18
The birth of celebrity — 19
P. T. Barnum and the 'freak show' — 20
Hollywood and the rise of the movie star — 21
Post-War fame — 23
The importance of television — 24
Stars today — 25
The Kray Twins and Louise Woodward: infamy as celebrity — 27
'Wacko Jacko': the freak show updated — 30
Conclusion — 31

3 The quest for fame — 33
Wanting it now: the case of Morrissey — 34
Explanations from psychological research — 36
Other theories accounting for the desire for fame — 43
Symbolic immortality — 49
Conclusion — 53

4	**Fame and the 'general public'**	**54**
	Television and psychology	55
	Cross-cultural research	57
	Reality monitoring and 'tele-literacy'	58
	Identification with people on the screen	60
	Parasocial interaction	61
	The formation of parasocial relationships	62
	'Public access' media	67
	Conclusion	71
5	**Identity crises: the perils of 'authenticity'**	**72**
	'The self' in psychology	72
	Popular music and 'the self'	78
	Rock'n'roll suicide	81
	Commodification	85
	Conclusion	89
6	**The problems of being famous**	**90**
	New relationships	91
	The loss of privacy	96
	Explanations for fame	100
	Delusions of grandeur: 'We're like God'	102
	The 'gift': all we want to do is make records...	104
	Preparing for fame	107
	Conclusion	108
7	**A taxonomy of fame**	**109**
	The typology of fame	110
	Levels of fame	116
	Fame trajectories	119
	Memorable characteristics of famous people	120
	A test of the typology	122
	Uses of the taxonomy	126
	Conclusions	127
8	**Beyond parasocial interaction: fans and stalkers**	**128**
	Fans	129
	Religious parallels	134
	Meet the fans!	139
	Stars in danger	142
	Conclusion	145

9 Postscript: the future of celebrity	**147**
Technological change?	148
Appendix: Possibilities for future research	155
Notes and References	158
Bibliography	177
Index	184

List of Tables

7.1	Types and levels of fame, with examples	121
7.2	Frequency of mention for the twelve most popular celebrity names by category	123
7.3	Mode rating for each category for the 38 celebrities (and frequency of the highest category mode value for each celebrity)	125

Chapter 1
Introduction: defining fame and celebrity

Imagine, for a moment, that you are famous. Let's say you are a leading British female pop singer with a couple of number one singles and a Brit award under your belt, and recently you have been the topic of much tabloid gossip regarding drugs (partially true) and sex orgies (unfounded). You live by yourself in a West London maisonette.

It is a Sunday afternoon. You have spent the morning in bed, reading about yourself in the papers – the usual steamy concoction of half-truths, exaggerations and outright lies. An ex-lover has gone public about your sex life (quite flattering, this time). The afternoon is dragging on and you could do with another cup of tea. You go to the fridge and you suddenly remember you are out of milk, in fact you ran out of milk this morning and you have already put up with two cups of black coffee. But you really fancy a nice milky tea now. It is too bad; you will have to face the outside world.

You draw back the corner of the curtain, ever so gingerly (of course your house has seen precious little daylight this weekend, even though it is hot and sunny). There are only two paparazzi outside now. That's a relief – there had been 20 or so first thing this morning. You decide to risk it. You put on your shades and a hat (you really can't be bothered to make up lavishly for a bottle of milk) and you step out of the house.

Whoops! You didn't spot the two behind the bush. Out they come, snapping furiously. You smile as best you can as you slip into your car and undertake the long journey round the corner to the newsagents. The good thing is, they'll probably think you've gone for the afternoon now and will pack their things up and leave. When you reach the newsagents the coast seems clear. You are the only person in the shop. You find some semi-skimmed in the fridge and get ready to pay. But the newsagent wants a chat. He wants to know about the rumours regarding your affair with a Premiership football player – amicably, of course. You laugh it off, and quickly pay the money, but as you turn to leave a middle-aged couple enter the shop, expensive cameras hanging round their necks. They've spotted you, despite the disguise, and they want a picture, an autograph at the very least. They have blocked your exit, so you can't refuse, but suddenly you spot a gap and slip through. You reach the safety of the street, and then – horror! – a traffic warden has just slapped a ticket on your car, and the paparazzi, on their way back to the office, have pulled up alongside and are having a field day at your expense! It's gone horribly wrong; all you wanted was a cup of tea, and now you just want to scream...

What can it be like to be famous? The fictitious scenario described above is merely a snapshot of the kind of experiences celebrities endure day after day, year after year as we reach the end of the twentieth century. It is, in historical terms, a most bizarre phenomenon. How did we, as a society, get into this state of affairs? What might it be 'doing' to us? This book sets out to explore these questions – what it means for an individual human being to be famous, or a celebrity, why it is an experience that is both desired and regretted, why it seems to cause so much distress, and how it is reflected back to the rest of society in the form of 'fandom' and the psychology of the 'viewer'.

Some of these questions have already been grappled with by other writers. There are studies of the cultural meanings of celebrity; the history of fame; the evolution of the 'star system' in the cinema; the quest for 'greatness' throughout history; and the social impact of mass communication. All of this literature will be referred to throughout the book. However, apart from the occasional academic paper, the phenomenon of fame and celebrity has so far evaded the gaze of the psychologist. Why should this be, when 'fame' is a word on so many people's lips, and its 'effects' debated constantly in the media?

Part of the problem is that psychology, in its quest for scientific credibility, has, through most of its history, avoided probing into areas in which quantitative research would be difficult to undertake. If a psychological phenomenon can't be studied in the laboratory, yielding hard data that can be analysed statistically, it has generally been neglected as a potential research topic. Then there is the problem of recruiting research participants. It's hard enough dragging undergraduates out of the bar to take part in a five-minute memory study, let alone trying to gain access to celebrities, at the end of a queue of journalists offering free publicity.

Then there is a problem with psychological (and indeed much academic) research – that it tends to be *literature*-driven rather than *topic*-driven. If someone hasn't published a paper on your topic before, it is considerably harder to generate interest in your research. Even highly intellectual academic folk love to pigeonhole each other. 'What sort of psychologist are you?' is often the first question we ask each other. 'What is your *area*?' The assumption is that your 'area' is sufficiently well-trodden by previous researchers to be a worthy concern. In many ways, then, this book is intended as a starting point for a psychology of fame and celebrity that can snowball into a worthy 'area' over the next decade or so.

Fame and celebrity: definitions

It would seem sensible to begin by defining some terms. The terms 'fame' and 'celebrity' are not strictly interchangeable. As Chapter 2 will demonstrate, *fame* has a long and distinguished history. The term *'kleos afthiton'*, translatable as 'imperishable fame', can be found in Homer, and over the years has fluctuated in meaning. Different types of fame have been identified throughout history: fame as immortality, spiritual fame (in the eyes of God), worldly fame (in the eyes of the public) and, more recently, the fame of the moment. Historian of fame Leo Braudy, whose work I shall refer to extensively throughout this book, has in fact called for a 'moratorium' on the use of the word 'famous', arguing that it has been devalued in the modern era[1].

It is more common to refer to famous modern-day individuals as *celebrities*. There is some excellent research exploring the sociological and cultural implications of 'celebrity'.[2] The defining characteristic of celebrity is that it is essentially a *media production*, and its usage is largely confined to the twentieth century. Cultural critic P. David Marshall conducts a thorough etymology of the term, relating it back to the French *célèbre* ('well-known, public'), and the Latin *celere* ('swift').[3] The suggestion here is that celebrities are well-known (through the media) for nothing in particular, whereas the truly famous are in some way *deserving* of individual recognition. The celebrity has been defined, by Daniel Boorstin, as 'a person who is known for his well-knownness'.[4] The concept of 'celebrity' allows a TV show, like the BBC's *Driving School*, to focus on a hitherto unknown individual, such as Maureen Reece, a woman who had consistently failed in her attempts to pass a driving test, and thrust her into the public eye, so that within weeks she would become a 'household name' (talked about by members of the general public).

Other terms that have similar connotations through history include 'heroes', 'idols' and 'stars'. The last of these terms is undoubtedly linked to the media age, originating in Hollywood, and probably derives from the long-standing image of an actual star representing the individual, beginning with the comet that appeared in the sky shortly after Julius Caesar's assassination.[5]

Fame as a process

So should we, following Leo Braudy, abandon the use of the words 'fame' and 'famous' to refer to what is essentially a media phenomenon, a here-today-gone-tomorrow celebrity? I would argue not. Braudy's argument is part etymology and part nostalgia; it is as though we will wake up one day to find mass communication systems dismantled, and return to a society in which true greatness shines through the artifice of fleeting publicity. The historical evidence demonstrates quite clearly that fame has, to some extent, always been regarded as essentially *amoral* and frequently undeserved. As early as Virgil's *Aeneid*, fame was portrayed as a 'filthy goddess' that circulates rumour and establishes certain individuals in the public eye for no 'good' reason. Today's filthy goddesses, from the *Sun* to the *National Enquirer*, use the words 'fame' and 'celebrity' interchangeably.

What I propose here is that fame itself be seen as a *process* rather than a state of being, that can operate even in restricted domains. Once one is famous, then questions about merit and worthiness can be applied to the individual in question. Those questions would never be asked if it were not for the process of bringing the individual's existence into the public eye. How that process is achieved may well vary from activity to activity. The brutal reality of the modern age is that all famous people are treated like celebrities by the mass media, whether they be a great political figure, a worthy campaigner, an artist 'touched by genius', a serial killer, or Maureen of *Driving School*. The newspapers and television programmes responsible for their publicity do not draw any meaningful distinction between *how* they are publicised. In each case, they have achieved fame, however fleeting, and the process of achieving fame brings with it various related experiences which constitute the scope of the current project.

Furthermore, fame – as a psychological phenomenon – is about more than celebrity. While it may be impossible to separate the two when we speak of fame in a national or international context, it is nevertheless still possible to be famous in a localised way. Think about when you were at school (perhaps you *are* at school, or teach in one). You probably knew the names of all the children in your class. You may even remember where they sat, what they looked like, where their homes were. But what about the other classes in your year? How many children did you know in those classes? Chances are, you knew one or two, maybe because they lived near you, or knew your brother or sister, or your parents. But there were always one or two children in each year whom *everyone* knew, pupils and teachers alike.

At my junior school there were quite definitely *stars*. There was Joey, whom everyone knew because he wore a hearing aid and kept getting into trouble; a girl called Linda, who was constantly teased on the (contentious) grounds of poor personal hygeine; and a boy named Parrish (I can't remember his first name), who wore a perpetual sneer and was constantly getting into fights. Teachers would hold Parrish up as an example of poor behaviour; a model that we would do well to refrain from copying. The rest of us had very little to do with him because he wasn't in our class. He was simply the most famous boy in the year.

Fame can be achieved in other local ways too. There are many psychologists whom *I* would call famous, but the chances are *you* would never have heard of them unless you are a psychologist too. There are undoubtedly people in, say, equestrian circles whom horse fans would consider to be massively famous, but whose names would be entirely unfamiliar to you or me (unless you are a horse fan too). The priorities of the media or the dominant culture determines which spheres of activity are most likely to yield fame to the people within them. In Britain in 1999, there are huge numbers of footballers who are famous to the general public regardless of our interest in football. But there are no famous fencers. In America very few 'soccer' players are famous because association football is not a sport that commands much media attention. In some countries fencers, archers, and representatives of sports hardly ever played in Britain are as famous as footballers. Generally speaking, academics are not likely to be as famous as sports people; unless we appear regularly on television, our activities simply aren't visible enough, important enough, or as photogenic as the activities of people working in other fields. Nevertheless we can be famous to each other.[6]

Special people

I had the idea of researching the psychology of fame long before I became a psychologist. For several years I worked as a freelance journalist in London, interviewing pop stars for various magazines, a job that allowed a useful insight into the workings of the star system. The interviews themselves were relatively uninteresting; occasionally I would get the chance to meet someone witty or articulate, but much of the time it was a rather perfunctory exercise. One interviewee, a US soul singer, fell asleep during our encounter (jetlagged, his publicist assured me). Once a very minor pop singer walked out in the middle because he didn't like me discussing tabloid rumours. The singer of a well-known Scottish pop band (rightly) cold-shouldered me for getting my facts wrong. One or two people refused even to look me in the eye during the interview. When I did meet someone genuinely interesting, such as the white South African Zulu musician Johnny Clegg, my interview schedule had to consist solely of questions like 'Do you remember your first kiss?'. Other interviewers were less fortunate;

there were several who were on the receiving end of boots or fists on account of asking the wrong thing. What always surprised me was the way they failed to retaliate; however, once the journalist leaves the interview situation, it's clear where the power lies, and a violent reaction from a star always makes good copy.

The really interesting thing about pop journalism was the subsidiary (and subservient) industry surrounding the stars themselves. The entrance of a band or artist into their record company offices is like a papal visit. Those who can get near offer flattery: *'Love* the new single!' 'You'll have to see the pictures, they're fabulous.' Criticism only takes place behind closed doors out of earshot of the stars themselves. Outside the record company office – when a band is on tour, for instance – there are usually enough lackeys surrounding the stars to maintain the flattery. 'Roadies' (the people who lug equipment around) are ten-a-penny and can be hired and fired in the blink of an eye. Sitting at the same table as the stars at dinner is a great honour. No one interrupts a star, however banal the verbal content; the mildest of witticisms issued by one of the band is greeted with gales of laughter from the assembled company.

I once interviewed a number of record company publicists about their work for a London listings magazine. One, Stuart Bailie, had worked at Warner Brothers for a time, but left because he grew increasingly resentful at the outrageous demands made by the company's artists. On one occasion he, along with a number of other employees, was dragged down to a central London record store where a Warners band was performing a lunchtime showcase to a disinterested assortment of shoppers and tourists. Bailie and his colleagues were forced to stand there and clap along 'like seals at a circus'. He also described how, during a British tour by Cher, the head of press had to spend her Sunday afternoon frantically telephoning chemists throughout London so that a lowly record company employee could go and buy a tub of the singer's favourite face cream.

What is it about these 'special people' that has so many other people grovelling? It is certainly not 'talent', skill, or intelligence. Are famous people simply extremely popular individuals whom others feel uncontrollably attached to? Not at all; once the stars were gone, publicists would frequently let rip about what hideous creatures they were. What interested me, as a (then) amateur psychologist, was not the socio-economic structure that produced these bizarre and apparently insincere relations (although I acknowledge its importance), but the effect all this fawning and flattery must have on the stars themselves.

What it certainly produces is a lifting of behavioural constraint. The usual social conventions of politeness and courtesy are waived, even when the star stands to gain from the publicity. I once spent a whole day with a fellow journalist and photographer in a hotel lounge in Manchester waiting for the lead singer of a famous Motown soul group to get out of bed and be interviewed (it had originally been scheduled for late morning). In the end both myself and the other journalist were restricted to a joint ten-minute interview backstage after the concert. No other group of people would get away with such a flagrant disregard for social conventions.

The problem with pop music is that bad behaviour is part of the tradition of the art form. The astonishing rise to success of the Manchester band Oasis was initially fuelled by tabloid reports of the Gallagher brothers' frequent violent spats and, like so many rock bands before them, they attracted vast amounts of publicity by wrecking hotel rooms, bragging about drug-taking and upsetting members of the public. There is no chain of responsibility for pop stars; the worst that can happen is that the record company terminates the act's contract, in which case the act can usually get signed by a rival (as happened several times with the Sex Pistols in the late 1970s), or produce and distribute the records themselves (though this has never, to my knowledge, been the case). If the band is commercially successful, like Oasis, record companies stand to lose more than they gain if they try and discipline (or drop) their artists.

Then there is the role that the general public plays in keeping the stars in clover. The antics of bands like Oasis are met with general disapproval, and yet they continue to sell vast quantities of records. Male sports stars who assault their female partners (a regrettably common experience in the late 1990s) are given a hero's welcome by their teams' fans when they next appear in a match.

The relationship between the public and the stars is summed up by an extraordinary incident in London at the end of the 1980s, when the Hollywood actor Dustin Hoffman was appearing as Shylock in a West End theatre production of Shakespeare's *The Merchant of Venice*. It was by no means a showcase for Hoffman, since the cast as a whole was exceptionally strong, and the director was Peter Hall, himself famous enough even outside theatrical circles. One evening Hoffman was unable to perform through illness and his part was taken by an understudy. When this was announced, over half the audience left and claimed their money back, and what was left of the audience booed a perfectly competent performance from the understudy.[7] This tells us something, perhaps, about West End theatre audiences; it certainly tells us a lot about the power that celebrities can command, simply by *being someone* whose name and face are known to the world.

When you have that power over the people who employ you, it is no wonder you feel you have the right to behave badly. But power is a fickle attribute, and celebrity behaviour can, ultimately, be explained in terms of its costs. The boxer, Chris Eubank, once apologised for his notoriously unpunctual interview behaviour to a journalist: 'I do have a tendency of being late, but I don't mean to. Anyway, just think. One day I'll lose. And I'll have to be on time when I lose.'

Overview of the book

In order to shed some light on the psychological processes affecting stars, their admirers, and the general public, I have tried to incorporate research from a number of different areas. There is, for reasons explained earlier, relatively little 'pure psychology' in here, though this is perhaps no bad thing. Psychologists have frequently ignored research in other, apparently unrelated, disciplines which might have closed off blind alleys and opened up fruitful avenues of exploration long before the psychological research got underway. Furthermore, there is a strong argument for blurring the boundaries between psychology and other social sciences (as has already happened in areas such as computing [cognitive science] and psychobiology). Much of the 'psychology' studied in connection with television, for instance, has been carried out by media and communications researchers, and warrants a complementary literature within mainstream psychology itself.

Chapter 2 is unapologetically historical in emphasis. A sense of history is crucial for understanding any contemporary phenomenon: Michel Foucault's historical work on crime, madness and sexuality, for example, has changed the way (many) social scientists think about, and research, those topics. The historical work in the present area is especially pertinent, since in many respects the history of fame is the history of Western civilization. Our understanding of history is saturated with names and faces which represent social and political change as well as artistic and cultural development. Furthermore, what the poets, philosophers and novelists of yesteryear have said about human behaviour is as important as the work of any contemporary psychologist armed with the latest statistical software package. This chapter ends with a consideration of the way technological developments over the last hundred years or so have changed the face of fame and produced celebrities.

Chapter 3 simply asks one question: 'Why?'. What is so special about fame that it has been sought by so many for so long? There are a number of attempts to account for fame's appeal psychologically: might fame be predestined through an individual's personality? Such reasoning seems counter-intuitive, though, and I propose some alternative explanations.

Enough about the stars themselves; what about the public? In Chapter 4 I turn to the issue of technology, and examine the ways in which both large and small screen have brought us closer to celebrities to such an extent that we treat them – to some extent – as though they are real people. However, we are not fooled as easily as that, and the role of the 'active viewer' is discussed here (and at a later stage in the book).

Much psychological research has, for better or worse, been stimulated by an identified 'problem' that requires a solution. This may be the result of the medicalization of psychology, part of what sociologist Nikolas Rose has termed 'the psy complex', whereby psychologists are seen as mind doctors, deployed for the sole purpose of 'curing' individuals whose 'minds have gone wrong'. My interest in fame has been sparked by intellectual curiosity rather than any noble intentions of healing the sick or saving the human race. Nonetheless there are several features of fame and celebrity which are distinctly problematic, and part of this book's remit is to identify ways forward for more philanthropic research that might offer some palliative remedies. Chapters 5 and 6 dwell on the psychopathology of fame and celebrity, investigating specific instances, from ones where individuals have found life in the public gaze intolerable, to others where it is merely something to whinge about in interviews.

There is no doubt that, despite the blanket treatment of the famous as celebrities, there are distinct variations in the types of problem faced by stars, and in the experiences they have *en route* to fame. There is therefore a need for a taxonomy of fame, and in Chapter 7 I have suggested four basic types of fame that may be achieved, four different levels at which it may appear, which are to be considered along with the progress of fame across time, and different attributes of an individual to which fame may become attached. This chapter reports some preliminary support for the typology at least, through the findings of a study conducted at Sheffield Hallam University.

Chapter 8 returns to the relationship between the stars and the general public, but this time looks at places where the barriers have been breached, with particular regard to instances of *fandom*. Being a fan can produce a quasi-religious fervour that is frequently ridiculed and/or pathologized by the media. However, fandom does at least mean that our relationships with the stars can be consummated and become bilateral rather than unilateral. This is not always good news, though, as in the disturbing phenomenon of the celebrity stalker.

In the final Chapter (9), I return to an historical perspective to consider the future of fame and celebrity. What, if anything, will recent technological advances do to affect the media production of celebrities and the effects they have on the public? Will the phenomenon of celebrity be consigned to the twentieth century as the Internet opens up new vistas of experience? Or are computers just toys for boffins? Both sides of the argument are presented here. While this chapter may have an air of idle speculation, its theme cannot be dismissed lightly: if the history of fame is also the history of Western civilization, the future of fame may turn out to be... well, jolly interesting, anyway.

Chapter 2
'Mad for noblesse': fame through history

The history of fame is about nothing less than the history of *Western* civilization. It is also about the history of the *individual*, and therefore it is about the history of human psychology too. I make these grandiose claims not simply to sensationalize the material contained in this chapter but also in an attempt to step backwards and rearrange one's perspective from a time when individual human beings did not even have *names*.

It is hard to overstate how important named individuals are to the history of Western civilization. Imagine a school history textbook without any rulers or monarchs, influential thinkers, pioneering scientists, or revolutionary figures; imagine an artistic culture in which the artists of the paintings in a gallery are anonymous, nobody takes individual credit for poetry, music or philosophy; and there are no great plays and novels because they would mean nothing without the names.

Hand in hand with the history of the individual runs every political, cultural and social transformation of the last three millennia. Our major religions have individual human beings as their touchstones – Jesus, Mohammed, the Virgin Mary. Even revolutionary attempts to overthrow an individual-oriented economic system with a collective one have had individuals at the helm, be they Lenin or Trotsky. The reason we cannot imagine history without individuals is because it has always been written this way: 'In 1066 some bloke came over to England from France with an army and another bloke got an arrow in his eye' fails to capture the imagination in the same way as a story involving two named individuals.

The birth of Western civilization

History as we know it, then, took some time to begin, and probably human beings were very different before. A valuable reference here is Julian Jaynes's *The Origins of Consciousness in the Breakdown of The Bicameral Mind*.[1] Don't be deterred by the formidable-sounding title; it is highly readable and contains some fascinating insights into the development of ancient civilizations. Jaynes's basic premise is that what we today call individual consciousness emerged as an experiential phenomenon only in modern times – before, phenomena such as forward planning were attributed to divine intervention. For example, if you saw someone outside your house mistreating a child or an animal, you might decide to intervene by calling the police, the RSPCA, or even tackling the culprit yourself. Having done so, you would most likely attribute whichever decision you took to your own sense of initiative. Or you may attribute it to some other internal characteristic, such as your personality, or common sense. But the Ancients, according to Jaynes's theory, would have attributed this decision-making to the voices of their gods. He argues (and he is not alone) that the auditory hallucinations of schizophrenia are a latter-day throwback to this 'dual' consciousness of earlier times.

The birth of individual consciousness, according to Jaynes, can be traced back to the advent of *names*. He estimates this as being during the Mesolithic era, some time between 10 000 and 8000 BC. At this point the ice sheet that had covered most of the planet retreated and activities like hunting and other exploitation of resources became easier, leading to the development of more static communities. Giving individuals names intensified relationships, leading to the practices of burial and mourning of the dead. The first tomb, that of a king, has been dated at around 9000 BC, at Eynam, just north of the Sea of Galilee. The dead king appears to have been later worshipped as a god, and Jaynes argues that this point marks the birth of civilization.

Initially, the reputation of these individuals would have been spread orally – by travellers and story-tellers – beyond the immediate community. This process was significantly enhanced by the advent of *writing*. The stage in history at which the written word emerged as a form of communication has been cited by scholars as the beginning of many phenomena, both cultural and psychological, that we take for granted today. The main point about writing is that it allowed people to communicate *ideas* rather than the limited factual information expressed in carvings and pictures. In later millennia, the burial chambers and the tombs of kings began to feature inscriptions, outlining their great deeds in chronological order. Jaynes cites this development as the invention of *history* – the recognition of *time* as a significant means of ordering experience.

Concurrent with this development was that of the *story*. Ancient stories were passed through generations orally, until they became established elements of cultural heritage. In Greece, around 500 to 400 BC, these stories found their way into written form, and marked a significant point in Western history, at which *literature* began to leave its impression on readers and to influence human activity. The epics of Homer (*The Iliad* and *The Odyssey*) created heroes out of legendary figures such as Achilles and Odysseus. As mentioned in Chapter 1, it was Homer who made the first mention of the concept of everlasting fame, and it was the practice of writing which preserved these heroic characters for future generations.

The origins of fame

Leo Braudy's *The Frenzy of Renown*[2] is the first port of call for anyone interested in the history of fame. It gathers together a vast array of archival sources and traces fame through literature and social history to the twentieth century. I shall endeavour to condense Braudy's arguments into a few pages, but this is only to skim the surface of what is a formidable body of work.

Braudy identifies Alexander the Great as 'the first famous person'.[3] He was not the first person to seek honour and glory through military exploits, but he was the first to claim all the glory for himself as an individual, rather than the perpetuation of a dynasty. Alexander was driven by the exploits of the Greek heroes and other legendary figures; his ambition was to emulate the deeds of immortals, and he succeeded.

The iconography that surrounded Alexander elevated him to one of the immortals alongside his legendary idols (as we shall see, famous individuals have always started out as *fans*). His appearance is best known from sculptures and coins, typically portrayed with a flowing mane of hair and eyes cast towards the heavens – a posture mimicked by Hollywood actors and pop stars many centuries later. He himself had become a model for later fame-seekers.

However, it was the Roman era which really fostered the rage to be famous, '[infecting] the world with the desire for personal recognition'.[4] Rome's function in the history of fame is as the first city-state, bringing together large numbers of people in close proximity so that being seen and being known are highly important qualities for an individual. Suddenly words like *fama* and *celebritas* were part of the vocabulary, and the recognition of civic honours was possible, even for someone who was not born into leadership (although the possibility of fame was still restricted to the upper classes). This enabled someone like Cicero, a Sicilian magistrate, to enter Roman society and work his way to the top of the ladder.

Unlike other famous Romans, Cicero was driven towards fame purely out of individual ambition; a non-Roman, he had no particular interest in achieving great deeds for the honour of the state. He simply chalked up 'honours', like modern sporting trophies, until he had achieved all that were possible. In many respects Cicero can be seen as the godfather of modern politics, pressing the claims of oratory over that of military leadership, since it is more suited to civic fame. Later, Augustus used coinage to publicize his image – along with appearing on coins, he had them inscribed with slogans such as *aequitas Augusti* ('the fairness of Augustus').[5] (The value of coins as publicity vehicles may have been a major factor in the role of money as a major political tool.) Augustus also became the first famous person to be associated with an item of clothing, making the toga standard wear for Roman citizens.

But Roman fame was not to everyone's taste. A man named Jesus Christ was simultaneously carving out a legend of his own through the 'miracles' he was performing to increasingly large crowds; unlike Cicero and his fellow exhibitionists, however, Jesus turned his back on worldly fame, rejecting Roman behaviour as vulgar. For Jesus, fame meant recognition of his message and the preservation of the spirit: 'his fame is not a fame for action but a fame of being'.[6] Later on, St Augustine made an even more explicit break with worldly fame, recognizing God as the only worthwhile audience for his deeds, and casting a mould for holy men and hermits for years to come. Braudy characterizes this period as the beginning of democracy, at least in spiritual terms – all are equal in the eyes of God. The privileging of the 'soul' of the most humble citizen gave a new significance to the individual human being. Now it was not just leaders and rulers who were important.

Fame through art and literature

For several centuries, fame meant little in Western society, with most of Europe under the strict control of the Church. During the Middle Ages, however, a number of factors combined to change all this – the invention of the printing press, the use of engraving to portray the human face rather than religious imagery, and the population explosion leading to increasing urbanization.

The most significant effect of these developments was the emergence of a literary culture. In line with earlier writers, poets such as Dante and Chaucer returned to the desire for fame as a dominant theme in their work. Dante's *Divine Comedy*, for example, 'stands out for its constant preoccupation with adjudicating who deserves to be remembered, for what reason, and in what way'.[7] Like Virgil in *The Aeneid*, Dante distinguishes between the worldly fame that is spread by rumour (*romore*, or 'noise'), and true, lasting fame. This polarity, argues Braudy, stems from the rise of the art as the expression of individual genius, where style is more important than content (that is, creative art can be traced back to the individual creator rather than the subject of the art). As a result, Dante's task is to decide the order of merit: 'Once Cimabue thought to hold the field/ as painter; Giotto now is all the rage/ dimming the lustre of the other's fame' ('Purgatorio' xi, 94–6).[8]

Chaucer makes no such distinction. He is the first author to portray fame explicitly as a *process*, conceding that even wickedness can earn one recognition. In his poem *The House of Fame*, he observes in a dream a vast hall on top of a rock, outside which are gathered the many people demanding fame – 'moo than sterres been in hevene' (line 1254).[9] The by-now-egalitarian nature of fame is clear in that this represents all sections of the population: 'But though they nere of no rychesse/ Yet they were mad for gret noblesse' (1423-4). Inside the hall are nine groups of people, each representing a different type of fame, in what practically amounts to a taxonomy. Each group is petitioning the goddess Fame for recognition. Some express a wish for fame for doing good works ('noble gestes'), and are rejected, while others receive her blessing despite having done nothing, or worse than nothing. Fame has no principles or morals.

As cities grew and publishing spread, it was becoming steadily easier for individuals to achieve fame during their lifetime. Although most books had a mainly religious content, the emphasis was gradually shifting to specific authors' interpretations of religious texts; furthermore, the trend towards individualism in society was hastened by the figure of the solitary reader. Books, rather than oratory or preaching, acted as a direct line between the individual and God's messages. As private publishers were set up, there was a move away from religious and royalist literature to 'a battleground of rival heroic families and genealogies'.[10] Meanwhile, Erasmus became the first celebrity author, travelling across Europe to publicize his own version of spiritualism.

Another major development at this time was the rise of portraiture and engraving, allowing 'the individual face...[to be] taken directly in the midst of life'.[11] In England, Henry VIII broke from Rome, embarked on wholesale destruction of religious images and promoted the secular art of portrait painting. Naturally he is the earliest famous person to become immortalized visually, in Hans Holbein's now-familiar picture. Soon, according to Braudy, 'faces were appearing everywhere',[12] and this enabled the famous to multiply the amount of recognition they could achieve.

In the Renaissance period, a new vehicle arose for creating fame: the modern theatre, which was attracting crowds not seen since the Roman era. Now, in addition to words and pictures, individuals had new means of self-presentation, and theatre itself became a powerful political tool. Notably, it began to threaten the monarchy by representing the monarch as an individual with a psychology rather than a divinely selected ruler. Later political developments such as the French and American revolutions helped to democratize fame further, '[creating] a potent free market of fame, in which the use of media – writing, painting and engraving – becomes a lever to power'.[13]

The dandy and the fraud

New kinds of famous person began to emerge during the eighteenth and nineteenth century. In America, Benjamin Franklin promoted the image of 'self-made man', emphasizing the individual's ability to navigate his or her own course to fame. In Europe, Rousseau sought 'fame for naturalness, a fame for inner qualities, for what one is without the overlay of social forms'.[14] But with the increasingly *public* nature of fame, he found this difficult to attain, being forever torn 'between his urge to be recognized and his urge to retreat'.[15] In this way, Rousseau acts as a model for many later, and more tragic, celebrities. Soon Byron and Napoleon were establishing their own traditions of fame, as the possessors of sheer glamour. Despite their popularity they also cultivated the art of aloofness. In England the fashion designer Beau Brummell invented the cult of the dandy, tying his tie 50 times to get the right look, and scoffing at others' dress sense (including that of the Prince Regent).

Along with prototype celebrities came new types of fame. William Henry Ireland set himself up as the discoverer of literary relics, such as previously unknown Shakespeare plays and letters; many celebrated scholars were duped, including Boswell and Sheridan, until he confessed all. Nevertheless, the fakes remained on display and he made some money from selling reproductions of them.

The realization (following Chaucer) that fame is not always accomplished through worthy deeds led Ireland's contemporary William Caulfield to publish a rogues' gallery named *Blackguardiana*, in which a variety of notorious and/or eccentric figures were honoured, such as famous pickpockets. The spectrum of fame was rapidly changing: in Braudy's words, 'the old distinctions between bad fame on earth and good fame in eternity were becoming hard to maintain'.[16]

Braudy clearly laments the old, 'good' fame, deriding the 'fame of the moment' brought about by 'immediate communication', and the importance of both performance, and the body, for fame in the twentieth century, both vestiges of a visual culture. But his research is important for charting the evolution of fame up to the present time and shedding so much light on the way that not only fame, but the history of Western culture, has been transformed through time.

The birth of celebrity

The two outstanding works on the phenomenon of celebrity are Joshua Gamson's *Claims to Fame: Celebrity in Contemporary America* and P. David Marshall's *Celebrity and Power: Fame in Contemporary Culture*.[17] The use of the word 'contemporary' in both titles indicates that both authors are concerned with applying their research to the here-and-now, although Gamson's approach is more historical, tracing the evolution of celebrity from the early Hollywood studios through to the machinations of the modern star system. Much of his research has focused on the 'gatekeepers' of celebrity culture, such as publicists, and the star-fan relationship (which will be discussed in more detail in Chapter 8).

Marshall, a cultural critic, takes a neo-Marxist approach to celebrity, examining the way that the capitalist system uses celebrities to promote individualism and illusions of democracy (the 'anyone can do it' myth). This is achieved through the cathartic role played by public access media, such as the 'chat' or 'talk' show, which can give the general public a voice (albeit one which is overridden by the formation of personalities such as Oprah Winfrey), and by the fact that celebrities are human beings. 'The cementing character of the negotiation is the basic and essential authenticity that a "real person" is housed in the sign construction'.[18] In other words, the fact that the celebrity is ultimately a symbol manipulated by the dominant culture is obscured by the reality that a human being lies at the centre. On the one hand, we adore celebrities as representing success and achievement; on the other, we ridicule them for representing 'false' values of commodity and exchange.

In a sense, Marshall's argument is not so different from Braudy's, with money entering the equation. Not only is modern-day fame devalued by the speed of communication and the short space between the deed and the recognition, but also by celebrities' relationship with profit-making organizations such as record companies, television channels and film studios. How can someone be truly 'great' when they perform for profit – and somebody else's profit at that? The continual tension between stars' desire for authenticity and their socio-economic role as a commodity lies at the heart of many celebrity dilemmas, as will be discussed in Chapter 5. In the meantime, I shall attempt to chart the rise of the celebrity in Western cultural history.

P. T. Barnum and the 'freak show'

If celebrity is essentially a media production, rather than the worthy recognition of greatness, then its purest form must exist through the powers of *hype*. Hype in its truest sense must have no object of any value; of course, great writers and performers have never been averse to a spot of good publicity, but hype implies that a phenomenon can be made to appear valuable, even when its value is non-existent.

Enter Phineas T. Barnum, the pioneer of modern advertising, the publicist who turned hype into something approaching art. Barnum made his name through the organization and publicity of what became known as 'freak shows' at which people with physical abnormalities were exhibited, usually being required to put on some kind of crude performance to assembled spectators. Freak shows were highly popular throughout the West during the nineteenth century; very often they were little more than human zoos.[19]

P. T. Barnum will not be remembered for his 'exhibits' alone but for the way he sold his shows to the public. His first triumph was an African–American woman named Joice Heth, an ex-slave who, it was claimed, was 161 years old and had been George Washington's nurse. The initial publicity was enough to draw in the crowds; but Barnum's master-stroke was to issue an anonymous letter to the newspapers in which it was alleged that, rather than an exceedingly old human being, Heth was nothing more than 'an automaton, made out of whalebone, india-rubber and numberless springs'.[20] Needless to say, the audiences soon returned to take another look. After Heth died, a physician estimated her age at 80; Barnum claimed ignorance.

Many of Barnum's 'exhibits' became out-and-out celebrities as the century wore on, earning more money than the average actor.[21] This led to a debate over the 'career' status of the people involved: were they appearing of their own volition, or were they merely unwitting victims of exploitation? Similar arguments can be heard today concerning the autonomy of topless models. One example of a genuine celebrity emerging from

Barnum's shows is Charles Sherwood Stratton, otherwise known as 'Tom Thumb', a dwarf who had been exhibited since the age of five (with parental permission), became relatively affluent, and was introduced to 'important people' despite, apparently, having limited performing talent. Indeed, as his career progressed, Stratton restricted his 'performances' to public appearances. Despite such apparent career control, he was still subject to an apparently arranged 'marriage' to a female dwarf and exhibited with a bogus child ('little Thumb'). All of these were stunts devised by Barnum, eliciting frenzied excitement in New York.[22]

Ultimately Barnum's real 'show' was not the exhibition but the performance of the publicity, later documenting all the trickery in a series of autobiographical volumes. He coined the phrase 'there's a sucker born every minute', and his dictum has been followed by advertising agencies ever since.

Hollywood and the rise of the movie star

The American publicity machine was fully established by the early twentieth century. All it needed was a corresponding cultural phenomenon to feed it, and that was provided by the development of the moving picture. The earliest movie stars were secondary to the films themselves; not surprisingly, since the technology was spectacular and audiences were initially motivated by curiosity rather than 'human' interest. Similarly, the people who appeared in the films were referred to as 'picture performers' (as opposed to 'proper' stage actors) until around 1907, and even after that the term 'film stars' was preferred.[23] With a media hungry for sensationalist news, it was relatively easy for early film producers to peddle their wares. It soon became clear that there was an easy way to publicize films, and that was to create 'personalities' out of the stars.

Who can be regarded as the first genuine film star is a matter of some debate. Film historian Janet Staiger has challenged the assumption that it was the independent Hollywood studios that first promoted stars over and above the films they appeared in.[24] Some accounts have identified 'Little' Mary Pickford or Ben Turpin as the first true stars to be created in this way. But, for the Barnumesque publicity surrounding her, it is generally agreed that Florence Lawrence merits the title of the prototypical movie star. In 1910, she was known simply as the 'Biograph Girl' for her work with the studio of that name, which two years earlier had become part of the Motion Picture Patents Company. An independent promoter, Carl Laemmle, then signed her to his company IMP, and immediately announced the 'death' of the Biograph Girl in a press release. Three days later she was reincarnated as Florence Lawrence, complete with in-depth interviews and the disclosure of personal information previously suppressed by the Biograph studio.

After this, film studios realized the commercial potential of creating stars, and each leading studio signed a leading actor or actress rather in the manner of modern football clubs snapping up the latest talent. These stars had an attachment to their studios that was similar to footballers and their clubs today, in that they were under contract in ways that (ostensibly) constrained their off-camera activities. Myrna Loy, for example, admitted to a magazine journalist that: 'I daren't take any chances with Myrna Loy, for she isn't my property... I couldn't even go to the drugstore without looking 'right' you see... I've got to be, on all public occasions, the personality they sell at the box office.'[25]

Studios took a lot of trouble to publicize their 'stars', using in-house publications as well as billboard advertising and, eventually, 'fan magazines', which carried in-depth articles on Hollywood personalities. 'While Ginger Rogers explained "why I like fried potatoes", Hedy Lamarr spelled out "Why a husband should be made to shave." '[26] It has been argued that this type of publicity constitutes the true essence of stardom: 'Actors become stars when their off-screen life-styles and personalities equal or surpass acting ability in importance.'[27] Eventually it was not just movie stars who got the star treatment; even Mahatma Gandhi's favourite dinner made it into the pages of the fan magazines, thus setting an important precedent for the modern era of celebrity. Today, magazines like *Hello!* and *OK!* focus exclusively on celebrities – from politicians and sports stars to film stars, pop stars and TV personalities – picturing them in their luxury 'hideaway' homes (if they haven't got one of those, the magazine will arrange for a photo shoot to be carried out in the grounds of a stately home), and discussing intimate details of their domestic lives. If there are children, they are a major part of the publicity too; if the celebrity's partner is also a celebrity, so much the better.

Post-War fame

Hollywood and the birth of celebrity acted as a blueprint for the fame explosion which has occurred during the second half of the twentieth century. Beyond the United States, the significance of the post-war period is the way in which celebrity became decentred from Hollywood. Before the 1950s, in most countries, 'fame' was still the preserve of political and military figures, and leading players in the arts and sciences, although the gradual spread of news media – newspapers and radio – was starting to focus more and more attention on members of the public involved in news stories.

One example of this is the case of Derek Bentley, a 19-year-old Londoner who was hanged in 1953 following the fatal shooting of a policeman during a bungled robbery. At the time of the incident there was a national debate in progress on the topic of capital punishment and Bentley became a *cause célèbre* for abolitionists, largely because his death was widely regarded as a gesture on behalf of the legal system, since Bentley's accomplice, who fired the fatal shot, was too young to hang. Indeed, 46 years later, the original conviction was overturned and Bentley received a posthumous pardon. Such was the publicity surrounding this case (and that of Ruth Ellis, hanged in 1955) that the chief hangman, Albert Pierrepoint, also became famous. It has since been suggested that he quit his post not, as argued at the time, as an anti-hanging protest, but because he stood to earn a large sum by selling his memoirs to the press.[28]

The Bentley story was one of the first news items to be spread simultaneously to a large audience by newspapers and television alike. As the 1950s progressed, the popularity of television made this the dominant medium for creating celebrity and disseminating information. Before then, radio had made an equally significant impact as a medium for creating stars. Above all, radio had been instrumental in creating the illusion of 'national identity' – a common cultural community into which it was easy to assimilate new styles of broadcasting and, with them, new types of celebrity.[29]

One of the most important features of fame Hollywood-style, as well documented in the literature cited thus far, was the invention of the close-up shot, pioneered by D. W. Griffith, who directed what is now regarded as the first-ever full-length feature film, *Birth of a Nation*, in 1915. The close-up enabled audiences not only to see the facial features of the actors but also their portrayal of emotions, thus intensifying the intimacy between star and spectator.[30] The advent of sound added another dimension to the star–fan relationship. Now viewers could not only see their idols in considerable detail, but hear their voices too. Similar developments were to occur in the recording of popular music.

> Initially, the invention of the microphone as an aid to recording favoured a relaxed style of singing, which heightened the nuances of 'personality' in each singer, rather than the rigorous technical perfection of the operatic tradition; whereas in the past one became a famous personality through the performance of extraordinary deeds, the recording artist became known to hundreds of thousands simply through 'being' on record. The emphasis changed from what one 'did' to what one was 'like'. (Buxton, 1990, pp. 429–30).[31]

The importance of television

Nothing, however, could compare as a vehicle for fame with the most important invention in cultural history, television. Television's rise in the 1950s completely transformed the relation between the stars and the general public. Prior to the popularization of television, stars were people you saw in special, somewhat distant, settings. You had to go to the cinema to see Laurel and Hardy, and to a cricket ground to see Bradman or Larwood playing. Television brought the stars into the home, so that you could sit a few feet away from Marilyn Monroe and Elvis Presley. Not only did television act as a vehicle for decreasing the distance between the public and already existing movies, news and sports events, but it began to create events of its own, and technological innovation occurred simultaneously, at a rapid pace. The invention of the video recorder has helped push things along even faster. The difference between programmes made in the early 1980s and those of the late 1990s is remarkable in terms of the increased sophistication in both style and content. The proliferation of soap operas, with naturalistic characters and storylines, and fly-on-the-wall documentaries and chat ('talk') shows with the focus on the general public, has taken us far beyond the star system set up by Hollywood, into an ever-increasing era of intimacy between viewers and the viewed.

Stars today

There is little doubt that the phenomenon of fame, transformed through media technology into celebrity, has created a common Western culture today which is, historically, highly unusual. The sheer number of famous names and faces is without precedent. As media outlets (newspapers, magazines, TV channels) increase in number there is a concurrent increase in the number of 'special people' who provide so much of their material. And even the people who work within these media become famous, often deliberately so.

The ultimate modern celebrity is the member of the public who becomes famous solely through media involvement. The subjects of major news stories have always achieved fame, however inadvertently (from Jack the Ripper to James Bulger). However, the nature of modern television programming is such that ordinary people, with whom the majority of viewers have an affinity, can become 'stars'. Maureen Reece, the spectacularly bad driver, was mentioned earlier; to her name we can add Eddie 'The Eagle' Edwards, a British ski-jumper who made it to the Winter Olympics but was exposed as hopelessly inept by superior competitors, yet remained cheerful amid this humiliation and was thus fêted by journalists covering the Games as symbolizing the mythical 'British spirit'.

We can also add the names of even more fleeting stars, individuals who have attracted media coverage for a few weeks but are swiftly forgotten as the well of stories runs dry. One such example is Paul Nolan, a window cleaner from Dorset, who appeared on the Granada TV series *Blind Date* in the mid-1980s. At that point the series was relatively new, yet highly popular, and the contestants had not quite mastered the audience manipulation tactics which have since become standard practice. When Nolan unveiled his (reasonably accurate) impersonation of the entertainer Bruce Forsyth the audience were in stitches, and it soon became clear that he was the most popular contestant since the show began. In between appearances, it was discovered that he was not as 'single' as one might expect a contestant on a dating show to be, and following several articles in the tabloid press, Nolan was dubbed 'the *Blind Date* rat', thus attracting further media exposure. In the meantime, the producer of an ailing ITV pop show, *The Roxy*, had taken the decision to recruit celebrity presenters in an (unsuccessful) attempt to boost its flagging audience. Following Nolan's elevation to celebrity status, he was invited to present the show one week along with Emma 'Wild Child' Ridley, the teenage sister of a minor television personality who had created a flurry of tabloid interest through her outrageous behaviour in London's clubland. The show was a disaster. Neither celebrity was able to sustain a rapport with the camera; Nolan was exposed as a one-trick pony, endlessly recycling his Forsyth impression, and he vanished from the limelight overnight.

The examples cited above could be construed as typically contemporary in that they exemplify the superficial nature of modern celebrity; people who have 'achieved' relatively little are thrust into the media spotlight with unseemly haste, are rapidly found wanting of any worthwhile qualities and are consigned to obscurity. But what about the modern-day inheritors of what Braudy proclaims 'true', everlasting fame? Surely contemporary culture produces as many highly talented individuals who are worthy of the recognition? The difficulty is that the star system operates the same way for a modern novelist or political figure as it does for a useless driver or *Blind Date* 'rat'. To become famous in 1998 beyond one's immediate field of excellence requires becoming a celebrity as well. But the *kind* of celebrity the media requires may not match the seriousness of the activities individuals are engaged in.

To put this in some kind of perspective, I quote here from the diaries of the British left-wing Labour politician Tony Benn:

Monday 1 April [1985]
I have had five invitations to go on chat shows, because it's my sixtieth birthday on Wednesday. I suppose when you reach sixty the journalists think they can rehabilitate you as an eccentric, lovable old character. These shows would be entirely personal, nothing to do

with politics, and I would be presented as an attractive person if I was prepared to go along with it on their terms.[32]

In the period leading up to this entry Benn had been on the receiving end of some of the most vitriolic press coverage in the history of British journalism. Nevertheless the media were evidently quite happy for him to play the celebrity role if all serious content could be relinquished. Likewise, former chancellor of the exchequer Denis Healey describes in his autobiography how he rarely encountered public animosity after the TV impressionist Mike Yarwood had turned him into a figure of fun, by highlighting idiosyncratic mannerisms, gestures, and even inventing catchphrases (*'what* a silly billy').[33] A (neo-)Marxist reading of these episodes might conclude that television serves capitalistic ends by deflating seriousness and thus trivializing any resistance to the prevailing economic system. Of course, the way modern politics works through the media is far more complex than that![34]

The Kray Twins and Louise Woodward: infamy as celebrity

As Chaucer pointed out as early as the fourteenth century, fame respects no morals or principles. With mass communication providing instant fame in a media-saturated society, the conditions are ideal for an individual to gain widespread fame (however short-lived) on the basis of notoriety. Across the world, people like Michael Ryan (the Hungerford shooting, the first of its kind in Britain) and Thomas Hamilton (Dunblane) have gained fame not only for themselves but for the locations of their acts. Whether the prospect of fame has acted as a spur for their activities is a matter for conjecture, but famous they undoubtedly are, whether we like it or not, and the media pontification on private motives – the 'state of mind' that produced the behaviour – serves to reinforce the primacy of the individual behind the atrocity.

Notorious individuals have always captured the public imagination, from despotic leaders such as Genghis Khan to the legendary highwayman Dick Turpin and the terroriser of Victorian London, Jack the Ripper. History softens their activities – Jack the Ripper now has a tourist trail devoted to him. The fascination with 'evil' and wickedness was bound to produce celebrities of infamy sooner or later, and the Chicago gangster Al Capone was probably the first to recognize the possibility of stardom available through notoriety.

The first self-consciously stylized criminal celebrities in Britain were Ronnie and Reggie Kray, twin brothers born in the East End of London shortly before the Second World War. Surrounded by the working-class poverty of the East End, the twins grew up in an environment in which crime and boxing represented the two local schools of excellence: 'In Bethnal Green boxing still seemed to offer a tough, determined boy the quickest way to fame and fortune.'[35] The Krays (Reggie in particular) were determined to succeed as boxers, but the sport was very sensitive to extra-curricular fisticuffs, and as the twins' reputation for violent street-fighting spread, that particular avenue was closed off to them, leaving only the criminal underworld as a potential vehicle for fame.

As with Alexander the Great, Ronnie Kray was, first and foremost, a *fan*: 'for years his dream-life had been peopled with successful gangsters, boxers, military men.'[36] To his collection of heroes he could now start to add the exploits of himself and Reggie, immortalized at last in the pages of the *East London Advertiser* for assault on a police officer. The twins kept a scrapbook in which this, and later exploits, were collected along with reports and photographs of their boxing triumphs. Before long, they had acquired a headquarters – a nightclub: now Ronnie had 'found his audience' and from there he could begin to emulate the deeds of his Chicago idols. As for Reggie, all he really aspired to was the 'good life' – so long as the twins made money he would be happy. But Ronnie was essentially motivated by fame – hardly the fame of which Braudy would approve, but one with a keen sense of historical perspective.

During the 1960s, the Kray legend extended beyond the East End to all parts of the country. This was partly a reflection of the 'high society' now kept by the twins as a result of their business activities, notably the homosexual relationship between Ronnie and a well-known peer, Lord Boothby, which the tabloid press gleefully turned into a scandal in the tradition of the then-recent 'Profumo affair', which had played a major role in defeating the previous government. It was all the twins needed to achieve national fame, and while it earned them great power within the

London criminal underworld, it also highlighted their activities to the law courts, and by the end of the decade – several grisly incidents later – they had both received lengthy prison sentences.

Like Barnum, the Krays' fame was achieved not for what they did but the way they used their activities to promote themselves. Unlike the traditional villains who suffered at their hands, the twins were a *performance*, staged for the benefit of the media; and *how* the media lapped it up!

It seems a strange leap from the contrived infamy of the Krays to the twists of fate that established Louise Woodward as a celebrity in the late 1990s; but their cases are linked in that, like the Krays, Woodward has achieved fame for the worst possible reasons. A British teenager working as a children's nanny in the US during 1997, Woodward was initially convicted of the murder of a baby boy in her care, with the verdict being overturned in favour of manslaughter when intent could not be established. The case was picked up by the world's media when the trial was broadcast live on American television. It had all the ingredients for a classic media 'soap opera': grieving parents, an otherwise very 'ordinary' defendant, ambiguous evidence.

In Britain it managed to provoke a typically xenophobic outcry – and not only from the tabloids – about Britons tried abroad, playing heavily on Woodward's image as a 'typical teenager' taking time out before university, who had been the hapless victim of circumstance. Woodward's return to Britain inspired a fervour rarely associated even with 'stars' – a press conference was arranged on her arrival at Manchester airport, and early morning television schedules were rearranged to allow live coverage. Her home village was swamped by reporters and paparazzi, much to the annoyance of the local residents (though they had not objected to their high media profile during the trial, when they loudly and unanimously proclaimed Woodward's innocence).

The irony of the situation was not lost on Woodward herself, who later told the audience at the Edinburgh television festival: 'I am not famous for anything good... people ask me to give autographs and sign baseball caps... [they] are not able to distinguish between notoriety and celebrity.'[37] Every day after her release, she claimed, she had been telephoned by journalists, asking her about which university she was hoping to attend; she had even been photographed by paparazzi while on holiday. 'I try to say that I'm a normal 20-year-old trying to lead a normal life but people won't let me.' Even without the slightest interest in achieving celebrity status, we can still have worldwide fame and recognition thrust upon us.

'Wacko Jacko': the freak show updated

From Barnum's scams to Louise Woodward's unwanted celebrity, the individual's ability to control the spread of his or her fame has declined in inverse proportion to the growth of the media. Even Barnumesque stunts have a habit of failing these days as advertisers need continually to dream up new ways of promoting products. Nevertheless, nothing draws in the crowds like a good old-fashioned freak show, and the tabloid press continue to delight in 'human interest' stories of disfigured individuals who have their faces rebuilt, the separation (or otherwise) of 'Siamese twins', and the agony of cosmetic surgery mishaps. Television cameras invade hospital operating theatres to capture life-threatening surgery, showcasing the skill of the medical profession. The rise of the visual culture of the twentieth century has, as Braudy argues, directed the media spotlight on to the body as never before.

What do you do when you are born into fame, and have become one of the world's most successful entertainers before you reach adulthood? Child stardom has never been easy to come to terms with in adulthood, as many Hollywood child actors later found to their chagrin.[38] For Michael Jackson, adulthood brought with it a new kind of fame: from being the world's most famous pop star he single-handedly reinvented the old-style freak show, playing on the media's obsession with the body. Throughout the 1980s and 1990s Jackson's career has been lived out on the pages of the world's newspapers as much as on the stages of its auditoriums. The plastic surgery (seemingly obligatory for modern American stars), the gradual lightening of the skin to produce a 'Caucasian' pigmentation, and the alleged drug-taking to preserve his falsetto voice, all contributed to Jackson's 'enfreakment' during this period.[39]

There were other stories. The *National Enquirer* carried pictures of Jackson apparently sleeping in a 'hyperbaric chamber' in an attempt to preserve his youth, like Lenin in his coffin; his building of a shrine to the actress Elizabeth Taylor; and eventually his arrest for alleged sexual assault on a young boy visiting his estate. (The subsequent media coverage of the investigation drew heavily on police examination of Jackson's body, largely in response to claims from the defendant that his lower body was a different colour to his face. The case was eventually settled out of court.) To provide a direct link to the freak shows of the nineteenth century, there was even a story that he had offered a London hospital $500 000 to acquire the skeleton of Joseph Merrick, the 'Elephant Man' of earlier fame.

To what extent has Jackson been the unwitting victim of lurid and intrusive media coverage? The following comment comes from a biography, where Jackson is commenting on the question of his sexuality:

> The bottom line is they [the public] don't *know* and everyone is going to continue searching to find out whether I'm gay, straight, or whatever... and the longer it takes to discover this, the more famous I will be.[40]

Could it be that Jackson has masterminded his own publicity? It is claimed that he is only too aware of the P.T. Barnum legend, having been lent a copy of his autobiography. The 'hyperbaric chamber' story clearly seems to have been a scam cooked up by Jackson himself following an incident when he was badly burned filming a Pepsi commercial and briefly considered using one for treatment purposes (though his burns were not sufficiently bad to require it). The skin lightening, it is claimed, is used to cover up the disfiguring effects of patchy depigmentation caused by the skin condition vitiligo; but his choice of white (as opposed to brown) make-up has led to accusations that he is rejecting his African heritage.[41]

Even when the glare of the spotlight appears to be unacceptably intrusive, the desire for fame may continue unabated.

Conclusion

The purpose of this chapter has been, in the main, to set up the phenomenon of fame as a historical and cultural peculiarity.

The history of fame is really about the history of the cultural role of the individual. In earlier times, celebrated individuals were simply known by their names; then by artists' impressions, and later by photographs and eventually moving pictures and sound recordings. The proliferation of media for publicizing the individual has been reflected in a proliferation of celebrated individuals. As the mass media has expanded, so individuals have had to *do* less in order to be celebrated, albeit for briefer periods than earlier. Television, bringing famous faces and sounds into our homes, has created different kinds of celebrity from the original Hollywood stars; at the same time political and artistic figures have been moulded into modern celebrities. Sometimes that celebrity results in fame for reasons that are unpalatable, either for the public or for the people on the receiving end. But the overwhelming message from the history of fame is that, as a process, fame is beyond the control of individuals, and probably beyond the control of any democratic society. Curiosity always gets the better of us in the end.

Chapter 3
The quest for fame

What is it about fame that has made it so attractive to people throughout history? What drove Alexander the Great, Cicero, P. T. Barnum and Ronnie Kray to emulate their idols, establish their names in the history books and gain the worldly recognition of the present time? In this chapter I consider a variety of factors that might contribute to the individual desire to be famous. Some of these are established psychological theories applied to the subject of fame, while others are more speculative.

It is not known at the present time how prevalent the desire for fame might be in the general population. It could of course be that everyone harbours an intense wish to be famous but only a few realize that goal. It is more likely that a small subset of the population is inflamed with such a desire, and a substantial proportion of this set have their wishes granted. But there is no one-to-one correspondence between the desire for fame and its attainment, because so much fame is unwanted (Louise Woodward, for instance), and there are noted cases where the thirst for fame is unquenched (the poet Chatterton, for instance, whose story will be told in Chapter 5).

What is seldom clear is the nature of the relationship between the desire for fame and its attainment. All the evidence we possess for such a relationship are the retrospective accounts by famous people of how they came to be famous, and these may be of dubious accuracy. Hindsight can reinterpret an all-consuming thirst for fame at all costs into a spiritual or philanthropic mission; alternatively there may be some prestige value in claiming that fame was achieved systematically. Moreover, talk of wanting fame has declined in the twentieth century, since fame has acquired a vulgarity through the perceived low value of modern celebrity. If fame is represented by Maureen from

Driving School, or a TV weather presenter, then it is a pretty poor ambition to own up to when you have a genuine talent for sport or music or writing. The myth of the 'gift' allows us to cling on to the belief that we will, eventually, be recognized and awarded for our innate potential, without having to seek out cheap and nasty publicity. Nevertheless, the pursuit of fame for its own sake has not completely died out.

Wanting it now: the case of Morrissey

During the mid-1980s one figure managed to dominate the pages of the weekly British pop papers: (Steven) Morrissey, eccentric singer with Manchester band the Smiths, who was the answer to the editors' prayers – an interviewee who would pour out his heart to anyone with a cassette recorder, throw in outrageous comments at the drop of a hat, and whose band were consistently producing music worthy of press attention.

Morrissey (he rarely used his first name) deserves a place in history simply for trying so hard to be famous, and achieving his aim in the end. As a teenager, he became an obsessive pop fan, endlessly compiling lists and critiques alone in his bedroom; on leaving school, he hung around on the fringes of the Manchester music scene, sang in bands, wrote reviews for music papers and even compiled a book on US glam rockers The New York Dolls (it was eventually published and sold over 3000 copies). Like so many famous figures of the past – from Alexander to Byron to Ronnie Kray – Morrissey was a *fan* above all else.

By the age of 18, he was becoming increasingly hungry for fame, and a scribbled note from this period reads: 'I'm sick of being the undiscovered genius, I want fame NOW not when I'm dead.'[1] But it was not for another six years that this hunger would be satisfied, when he and fellow Mancunian musician Johnny Marr put together the Smiths and had a string of hit singles and LPs, attracting massive media coverage before splitting up in 1987. Morrissey embarked immediately upon a solo career, enjoying acclaim for a while, and continued to release records up to the end of the century, albeit with comparatively limited success.

Unlike most of his peers Morrissey was never reticent about the source of his career ambitions; as he admitted in a later interview: 'I always had a religious obsession with fame. I always thought being famous was the only thing worth doing in human life, and anything else was just perfunctory.'[2] This is a significant revelation, since it harks back to the myth of the 'gift' while at the same time suggesting that, irrespective of whether or not Morrissey perceived himself as possessing talent, he nevertheless demanded fame for its own sake. Any mode of expression – writing, singing, criticism – would do as a vehicle.

Similar stories? Blur singer Damon Albarn:

> When I was at school, I never had any interest in pop music... I was just on this big 'this-is-what's-gonna-happen' thing. I guess it's quite insane to say, from the age of 11, 'I know I'm gonna be great!' But that's what I did. People just laughed at me. (*Melody Maker*, 6 April 1991).

It seems that, for some famous people at least, the desire for fame is something of which they are aware from an early age. To return to the question posed earlier: is the desire for fame something many harbour, which some achieve and others not? Or are those with early ambitions for fame in some way 'destined' for it? Certainly Morrissey felt that this was the case: 'I always knew something, shall we say, *peculiar* was going to happen.'[3] Alternatively, fame may seem predestined because of some unusual feature of one's childhood; for example, the television presenter and model Rachel Williams:

> Since I was 10, I felt like I was headed for being in the public eye. I don't know where that comes from. My height. It probably has something to do with that. I always stood out. (The *Guardian*, 1 September 1996).

The desire for fame in any guise has strong historical traditions. A clear parallel with Morrissey is the French writer Jean Jacques Rousseau. As mentioned in the previous chapter, Rousseau ushered in a new era of fame, where the emphasis was on the inner qualities of the individual rather than one's self-presentation in society. If the self is the 'gift' one has to present to the world, then its form of expression is arbitrary: so Rousseau, like Morrissey, flitted from one domain to another – from Venetian politics to Parisian music – before settling down to become a man of letters. Morrissey's career was the reverse, beginning in solitude but ending in high visibility. Unlike Rousseau, however, and unlike some of his more tragic peers, he saw no paradox between being both a private individual and a public centre of attention.

Explanations from psychological research

What can psychological theory say about the desire to be famous? An important source here is the work of D. Keith Simonton, an American researcher who has published over 100 articles on the psychology of historical figures and theories of creativity and genius. Simonton describes his approach as the psychology of history, and his methods, along with painstaking archival research, involve some fearsome statistical analyses of historical material. In his book *Greatness: Who Makes History and Why*[4], he outlines a variety of theories that try to answer the question, which I will attempt to summarize here, along with other assorted theories and findings.

Biological inheritance: do genes play a part?

The study of 'bloodlines' linking famous individuals through their family trees was conducted as long ago as 1869 by Francis Galton, who identified a number of striking trails through various families, most notably the Bachs of Germany, who produced well over 20 musicians. He also argued that the more famous the individual, the greater the likelihood that he or she would have famous relatives.

Galton was thoroughly committed to the notion that genetic endowment is the major factor influencing human behaviour, later founding the eugenics movement (which attempted to block the spread of 'bad genes' through the population through social control). Some of his ideas have become fashionable again through the science of behavioural genetics, which seeks biological explanations for human behaviour. Much of the geneticists' evidence rests on the much-publicized cases of separated identical twins exhibiting remarkably similar behaviours in later life; indeed the Krays' biographer alludes to some of this work in attempting to account for the criminality of the twins.[5]

Quite apart from the absurd notion that 'criminality' is a universal, internal quality of an individual, the (identical) Kray twins are all the counter-evidence one needs to disprove the theory of biological inheritance. Inseparable from birth, sharing both the same genetic make-up and the same environment, we should expect them to demonstrate patterns of behaviour that are markedly similar. However, in his twenties Ronnie was diagnosed as having paranoid schizophrenia (argued by some to be an inherited disorder), and practised homosexuality throughout his civil life (likewise claimed to be genetically determined[6]), while Reggie showed no signs of *clinical* psychopathology and was also heterosexual.[7]

What about the blood lines of famous families? One flaw in Galton's research is that he failed to compare the inheritance of 'greatness' with the inheritance of any other similar traits. His fundamental error, though, is to assume that, like criminality, 'greatness' is a definable, universal human attribute that can account solely for success in the arts, sciences and other entirely *cultural* pursuits. He may as well have searched for bloodlines that predicted the inheritance of *toilet cleaning* as an occupation, and would undoubtedly have found similar patterns. It seems hardly surprising that there is a huge correlation between the career choices of parents and offspring.

As Simonton puts it: 'We should probably treat all psychobiological theories [of inherited greatness] with scepticism'.[8]

Psychodynamic explanations and the sublimation of the sexual instinct

Perhaps Freudian theory can shed some light on the psychological origins of fame. Freud never wrote about fame directly, although it is alluded to in his work on creativity, in which he argued that creative artists were primarily motivated by the desire for fame (along with wealth and romantic love). John Gedo, a practising psychoanalyst with a special interest in artists, claims that none of his clients have acknowledged the desire for fame and fortune as the primary motivating force behind their careers, and argues that there are much easier ways of obtaining the good life than struggling for artistic recognition.[9] This may be true in today's culture of instant stardom. John Milton was never in any doubt, however: '*Fame* is the spur that the clear spirit doth raise ... to scorn delights and live laborious days' (*Lycidas*, lines 70–2).[10]

Where Freudian theory may be at its most persuasive is in his later work, notably *Civilization and its Discontents*, where he develops the theory of 'sublimation': essentially, all human cultural activity is the 'sublimation of the sexual instinct' – to put it simply, we invented culture as a way of keeping our minds off sex. Why should we have chosen to do this? Freud takes in rather a lot of complicated explanations involving taboos and incest avoidance which have since been successfully challenged by anthropological research. It is also important to remember, as Julian Jaynes[11] has pointed out, that civilization needed the right physical conditions to flourish, never mind cultural tools such as written language and basic architectural principles. However I don't think we need to seek a more complicated explanation than the fact that culture has made it possible for us to attain the illusion of immortality. Why should so many great artists, writers and composers have been happy to settle for posterity rather than instant fame? Before the contraction of the globe into the mass media 'village', people could not expect to achieve fame in their lifetime, yet they were not deterred in their quest by this minor detail.

Personality factors: does fame require a special kind of person?

Earlier I described how people such as Morrissey and Damon Albarn appear to have had a strong sense of destiny at an early age. Could it be that fame is, to some extent, self-determined? Perhaps the likes of Rousseau flitted from vocation to vocation because something in their personality forever drove them in the direction of greatness? It seems unlikely; but perhaps there are certain characteristics common to those who achieve fame.

Simonton reports the findings of a number of studies employing variations on the Thematic Apperception Test (TAT), a widely used nomothetic test of personality, in which people are shown a series of 20 ambiguous pictures of human actors and are required to compose a story for each picture including 'before' and 'after' material. The psychologist then codes the responses according to a number of selected criteria, notably, power and 'affiliation' (the need for love or companionship).[12]

In one study a variant of the TAT method was used to analyse the inaugural addresses of American presidents. Truman and

Kennedy emerged as the most power-hungry, while Kennedy and Nixon scored highest on the affiliation measure (Roosevelt and Garfield were the lowest scorers). In general, high power-hungry scores were good predictors of the presidents' likelihood to engage in military conflict, while high affiliation scores predicted a tendency towards nepotism, notably the appointment of close friends or relatives to cabinet positions. Similar findings were achieved with analyses of the announcement speeches of presidential candidates and with analyses of Soviet politicians.

Simonton devotes a whole chapter of his book to the retrospective analysis of personality and its importance in determining greatness. He concludes that the personality characteristics most likely to produce fame are the drive to succeed (exemplified by the 'type A' pattern of behaviour), and the tendency to take risks (necessary for breaking new cultural and intellectual ground). Nothing startling there; elsewhere, his attempt to apply traits derived from psychometric tests to historical figures is rather more *descriptive* than predictive.

Once again, Braudy has the last word. While many great careers appear to have been masterpieces of long-term planning, he suggests that perhaps the most essential characteristic necessary for fame is a sensitivity to situation – the ability to improvise when planning fails.

> It may be in the nature of those who achieve the greatest fame that they can do both, subsuming the standards of the past and showing their insufficiency, yet at the same time responding in a spontaneous and instinctive way to the crisis of the moment, doing naturally and immediately what is necessary.[13]

Developmental factors

Simonton identifies three factors relating to family background that might contribute to the realization of 'greatness'. The least convincing of these is *early mental stimulation*, the argument being that a positive nurturant environment is a significant spur to future achievement, and that a 'love of learning' may be instilled in relatively affluent homes. This may be true, but like the role of schooling in producing greatness, when these variables are partialled out it is almost certain to be *social class* that emerges as the determining factor. It could be argued that affluent family backgrounds instil a more future-oriented time perspective in their children than do poor families, but this factor might only explain ambition in general, of which 'greatness' is only a small subset.

A counter-argument is that greatness may have been inspired by some *adversity* in early life. A general impoverishment of environment may be said to constitute 'adversity', but this theory relates specifically to some single trauma that leaves behind a scar and an urge to succeed in order to overcome the distress. Simonton estimates that well over half of a large sample of eminent historical figures lost a parent before the age of 30, and that nearly a third of all winners of the Nobel Prize for Literature lost a parent in childhood. Whether these compare with the average life expectancies of the periods covered is not disclosed. It has to be said that, even if early parental death *could* be found to predict later success, it is not a finding that parents would like their children to get wind of!

The most intriguing of the developmental theories suggested by Simonton is that of *birth order*. From a purely individualist (or genetic) perspective, this seems as haphazard a factor as the position of the stars at birth, or whether the month had an 'r' in it. But birth order has a major impact on the socialization of the child; if Freud was right, and infancy is a period during which one's essential character can be cast in stone, then the first-born has a special environment in which s/he is the absolute centre of attention and forms a unique parental bond: 'If a man has been his mother's undisputed darling he retains throughout life the triumphant feeling, the confidence in success, which not seldom brings actual success along with it'.[14]

The evidence for this theory looks quite promising: throughout history there has rarely been more than one sibling who achieves prominence, a trend that persists through to modern-day celebrities. Moreover, Simonton argues, first-borns do appear to have a higher success rate. Similar evidence was produced by Galton, apparently without it occurring to him that the heredity theory should surely predict a random distribution of greatness according to birth order. Adler later added a further, more plausible explanation: the first-born child desires fame and success because s/he needs to claw back the indulgent attention s/he received before the arrival of siblings.[15] This does not, of course, explain the success of only children. Simonton produces some evidence to suggest that later-born children who attain fame are more likely to be revolutionary figures or creative writers. But the net is cast so wide at this point that the argument starts to look somewhat tenuous.

Outsiders

Another explanation for 'greatness' suggested by Simonton is that it may reflect the desire for success in a culture within which one feels estranged. In Chapter 2 I discussed the case of Cicero, an outsider in the context of Rome, driven by his desire for personal glory rather than the glory of Rome. To Cicero we can add the (statistically) unexpectedly high number of Jewish Nobel Prize winners and, in more recent times still, the overrepresentation of Afro-Caribbeans and African-Americans in specific fields such as sport and pop music in Europe and America. Why should this be? It is possible that the intermingling of cultural backgrounds produces a fertile creative environment:

> Persons who have been uprooted from traditional culture, or who have been thoroughly exposed to two or more cultures, seem to have an advantage in the range of hypotheses they are apt to consider, and through this means, in the frequency of creative innovation.[16]

Another suggestion is that 'outsiders' within a culture may be driven to seek fame, particularly people who feel marginalized for reasons of sexuality. Simonton lists a large number of historical 'greats' who practised homosexuality, and there is little doubt that, in the fields of art and entertainment, the proportion of gay *men* in particular vastly exceeds that which would be predicted by the incidence of homosexuality within the general population. Simonton accounts for this in terms of 'unconventional life styles',[17] citing many examples of famous people who remained unmarried, and those who could never marry happily (like Bertrand Russell, who married four times). He explains this in terms of the 'autonomy' of the creative individual, which drives them to obsessive involvement in their work, leaving little time for romance, or even bringing up a family.

An alternative explanation for the high incidence of homosexuality in the arts and entertainment industries is that the prospect of everlasting fame through success in these areas may be a preferable alternative to preserving one's DNA through biological reproduction. But why not in other areas inviting fame and 'greatness'? The answer could be that, in more conservative domains, such as politics and sport, great pressure is exerted on individuals to conform to dominant norms and be seen with opposite-sex partners; political leaders are nearly always married by the time they come to power, and sportsmen and women frequently marry at an early stage in their careers.[18] The more individualistic domains of art and entertainment place fewer pressures on sexual conformity. I will return to this theme later in the chapter.

Genius and madness

Some of the most popular stereotypes of creative pioneers through the ages have been the portrayal of the 'mad scientist', the individual whose brilliance is such that s/he cannot relate to ordinary people, and of the 'tortured artist' whose creative flights of fancy are indistinguishable from his or her bouts of melancholy or mania. Cicero himself described the thirst for fame (*gloriae cupiditas*) as a 'disease'.[19] Could it be that the neurological preconditions for genius are closely related to those for psychopathology?

Simonton lists a huge number of creative geniuses who appear to have suffered from some form of psychiatric disorder. Some of these are very well documented, for example Schumann's manic depression, where his 'manic' phases enabled him to compose his best work, and van Gogh's depression which resulted in suicide. Alongside these, he also lists a number of famous individuals who have had psychologically disturbed relatives, suggesting that genius and madness can 'run' together in the same family.

Of course, one of the problems of investigating psychopathology across history is that we are having to rely on archival material to supply retrospective diagnoses of disorders which have only been identified in the last 100 years. It is easy to look through the biographical details of a famous individual and spot eccentricities which might indicate schizophrenia, or obsessive-compulsive disorder. It is quite another thing to diagnose mental illness in a modern clinical context. There are relatively few cases of historical figures seeking treatment for psychological disorders (although this may be due largely to different attitudes towards mental health across historical periods); however, we know that Rachmaninov visited a hypnotherapist, leading him to compose his most famous works (the second symphony and second piano concerto), and we also know that Hemingway underwent electro-convulsive therapy. A more recent study looked at eminent British poets, and discovered that half had either been prescribed drugs or given hospital treatment in order to cope with depressive disorders.[20]

What are we to make of this large body of evidence? A clue may lie in the solitary nature of artistic pursuits: poets, composers and painters seem to be the most frequently troubled by their private cognitions, but then they are alone with them for most of the time. More gregarious pursuits, such as acting and music, seem to have lower rates of psychopathology, and where it does occur, perhaps it is related more to the experience of fame than to any innate characteristics.

Rather than inspiring artists to creative heights, might not psychological disturbance be more likely to hamper their ambitions? Indeed, as Gedo points out, 'current psychopathology is very likely to *interfere* with creativity', citing the example of the sixteenth-century Florentine painter Jacopo da Pontormo, who, when commissioned to paint frescos for a chapel, was found to spend so much time 'lost in private cogitation... that through an entire day he might fail to make a single mark on the painting'.[21] In today's time-pressured society, it seems highly unlikely that a seriously psychologically disturbed individual would get very far in his or her chosen career. Correspondingly, as Simonton suggests, had psychoactive drug treatments been available in past centuries, we may have lost some of the great masterpieces of history!

Other theories accounting for the desire for fame

Simonton's research, however thorough, is restricted to explanations for 'greatness' as opposed to the desire for fame itself; in many respects, it can only account for the fame of those who succeed in obtaining it. He also, by his own admission as a psychohistorian, has concentrated on famous individuals of the past; there is a wealth of research potential for anyone interested in the psychological characteristics of modern-day celebrities. In the remainder of this chapter I shall outline a number of alternative theories which might account for why so many people desire fame.

Generativity: the urge to live on

The theory of generativity derives from the work of the American lifespan psychologist Erikson, whose 'eight ages of man' includes a seventh stage, in middle adulthood, which is characterized by a struggle between 'establishing and guiding the next generation', and the indulgence of self in the here and now. The former impulse is described as *generativity*.[22]

What forms might generativity take? A variety of possibilities have been suggested, from professional and voluntary work through to community and leisure activities.[23] At a reductionist level, generativity is little more than the urge to reproduce biologically, to live on through one's children; the Eriksonian model suggests that child-rearing is a subset of a more general desire to invest in the next generation, a kind of altruistic desire for the future well-being of the species.

Where does fame fit into all this? It could be argued that fame is another way of preserving one's identity for future generations. One possibility is that this is a way of defying death, and that the basic human desire for immortality can be realized in a symbolic sense.[24] John Kotre argues that cultural immortality is more likely to be desired in the post-reproductive stage – in other words, in later life.[25] In either case, the authors envisage cultural generativity as taking place at a much later stage than is the case with the vast majority of famous individuals. It may be that altruistic or philanthropic fame tends to occur later in life; however the theory of generativity does not by itself account for the desire for fame that appears as early as childhood. Viewed from an evolutionary perspective, however, Erikson's theory might, along with Freud's theory of sublimation, serve as a possible insight into how culture and the desire for symbolic immortality emerged.

Discourses of success

Leo Braudy has written of the 'inescapable imagery by which one lives life' that is produced by famous individuals' accounts of their upbringing.[26] Narrative psychology is a field which investigates the kind of life stories produced by individuals; researchers are not necessarily interested in the truthfulness of these accounts, but in the way that we use stories to construct meaning for our lives, and a sense of destiny.

The power of language as a tool for shaping our behaviour is the concern of many modern psychologists who study the way that 'discourse' (which can include anything from everyday conversation to symbol systems operating in society at large) works not only to create 'reality' but also to structure society by producing 'subjectivity', power relations, the 'right' to speak, and so on.[27]

How might the discourses of fame have contributed to the desire for fame through history? The deeds of Alexander, in emulating the gods, helped to create what Braudy calls a 'vocabulary' of fame which can be 'reproduced and defined by others'.[28] By bringing heroic deeds within the scope of human beings, he acted as a role model, fashioning a 'text' that could be rewritten by future generations. As history progresses, a proliferation of 'fame texts' emerge, covering different ways of being famous (from Chaucer to Capone) and different outlets of expression (from writing to performance). One only needs to look at the way in which famous individuals from Byron through to Ronnie Kray and Morrissey absorbed themselves in the legendary exploits of their idols to see how powerfully these texts can influence an individual's outlook.

Some of the discourses surrounding fame have become a permanent feature of the overall text of 'making a famous life' – most notably, Alexander's heavenward gaze, reproduced by countless twentieth-century celebrities in publicity shots. Other images, such as the tortured artist or poet in his or her solitary garret, have been carried over into pop music and are still present in the discourse of even the most public, performance-oriented celebrities. The myth of the 'gift', referred to previously, is one of the most successful of modern discourses.

How might these discourses work in producing a desire for fame? Clearly not in any direct way; they are just 'ways of talking' that float through society. Where they may influence behaviour is through the promotion of a value system constructed in numerous magazine and television features whereby recognition, financial success and achievement are represented as the positive goals of the dominant culture.[29] The term 'V.I.P.' to signify a celebrity is a typical device, elevating an individual above the general mass of humanity; depictions of the 'good life' in celebrity magazines is another, constructing the hideaway home and the happy nuclear family as the Holy Grail of human existence. Another discourse, that of the 'ordinary', or 'girl/boy-next-door' celebrity is closely related, presenting fame as a means of attaining a dream home and happy family for the most humble reader or viewer. It has been argued that such discourses may play an essential role in consumer society's manipulation of celebrity to maintain the image of democracy.[30]

At the same time, however, there are a significant number of discourses of fame emerging whose theme is the damage that fame can do to an individual – disillusionment, loneliness, persecution by obsessive fans and stalkers (Chapters 5 and 6 will focus more closely on the problems of fame). Given these counter-discourses, why is fame still sought by so many? Perhaps the positive aspects of fame appeal to something that is more deep-rooted than the fanciful notion that we can emulate our heroes.

Fame is sexy

Given the popularity of fame through history, and the tempting possibilities dangled before us in the mass media, what are the most appealing aspects of fame? What is it that really stokes the fire in the belly of ambition? In this next section I shall return briefly to the arguments of biological determinists and geneticists.

Joshua Gamson describes an (unreported) exchange between a journalist and a film star who, when asked why he got into acting, replied 'because there were a lot of pretty girls I wanted to fuck'.[31] A traditional sociobiological argument might go something like this: most of life (human or otherwise) is spent attempting to reproduce our DNA. That is the only identifiable purpose in life, and so most human activity needs to be interpreted in this light.[32] The attractions of fame are blindingly obvious: we crave fame because fame makes us popular, and brings us into contact with lots of people to make babies with. Quantity spawns quality, so both men and women stand to benefit from the reproductive advantage of being famous.

There is another huge advantage fame gives us in that respect; like power and wealth in general, it enables us in effect to transcend our inherited biological characteristics and compensate for any shortcomings in that department. We might be dealt a rotten pack of biological cards – physically ugly, endowed with a physique hopelessly inadequate for reproduction or attracting sexually receptive partners – and yet, by mixing with the famous and the beautiful we get to join their exclusive club with all the benefits of membership. Both Boswell and Rousseau admitted that the motivating feature of fame was for them the opportunities it opened up for meeting women.

If that were the case, how come so many celebrities *are* physically attractive? Why do they need the added advantage that fame brings them? One could argue that, in the period before this century – before the birth of celebrity – people were inspired to pursue an artistic career or a political quest as a means of becoming famous and transcending their lack of looks (there are suggestions, for example, that Byron sought fame to compensate for his club foot; however, as Braudy suggests, these may derive from a twentieth-century tendency to overrate the role played by bodily perfection in public life). Today, with visual media operating as the principal vehicles for publicity, being beautiful has become a *criterion* for fame, not a disincentive. Fame has evolved into a superficial cultural pursuit that is of little benefit to most of the people who attain it.

The 'gene pool' argument is unconvincing because it ignores the tremendous efforts individuals make to attain fame, their attempts to preserve it when threatened, and their willingness to endure the heavy costs of fame simply to remain in the limelight. And what of the desire for posterity, so strong in the precelebrity age? Many of us are still content with simply 'going down in history', regardless of fame's worldly attractions. Fame as a sexual strategy cannot, for example, explain why a financially and emotionally troubled hotelier should spend three months learning to fly in order to stage a high-profile suicide, as happened recently on the south coast of England. The pilot, Terry Brand, left a letter declaring: 'My full intention in learning to fly was to move on in one dramatic moment.'[33]

Fame and homosexuality

At this point I return to the theory introduced earlier, in an attempt to account for the over-representation (compared with the general population) of homosexuality in the arts and entertainments. Sociobiological explanations in general tend to fall apart once homosexuality is introduced into the equation (if ever there was a recessive gene it would be the hypothesised 'gay gene', and there are no signs of homosexuality's demise just yet!). Rather more convincing in this case is Erikson's theory of generativity, which allows for the possibility that human beings can achieve a sense of investment in the next generation through culture rather than biological reproduction.

But, you might argue, what about today's self-indulgent performances? How might, say, the fame of a supermodel or a DJ have any possible benefit for future generations? For the answer, I will have to invoke the notion of the 'selfish gene'[34] and argue that it is not enough simply to view culture as a rather nice philanthropic alternative to making babies. It may just as easily be a thoroughly self-indulgent alternative to biological reproduction, since the whole point of reproduction is the preservation of one's DNA. If we have no intention to reproduce biologically (and I am *assuming* here that this is true of most homosexual individuals[35]) then we must find some other way of preserving some essence of self.

Is there any historical evidence for this, apart from the mere prevalence of homosexuality in the arts? There is a very interesting passage in Chaucer's *The House of Fame* which, if my interpretation is correct, suggests that fame has always had a special appeal for a homosexual population. As the nine groups line up to appeal for the goddess Fame's approval, there is one group who have a curious request. They say they haven't really done very much, and are not popular with women (indeed, detested by them). And yet, they desire fame so that it can appear as if 'wommen loven us for wod' (like mad):

> Thogh we may not the body have
> Of wymmen, yet, so God you save,
> Leet men gliwe on us the name!
> Sufficeth that we han the fame.

(lines 1759–62)

In this passage they appear to be requesting fame for its own sake (read *gliwe* as 'stick'). But the interesting point is that they state explicitly that they are not interested in women's bodies; interested, that is, in having sex with them. For what other reasons should they wish to have the adoration of women? It does seem that the group Chaucer is describing here, although rather unflatteringly because they haven't actually achieved anything of note, is a homosexual group who desire fame for no other reason than the sake of posterity.

It may be that homosexuality is not the only reason for us to embrace fame as symbolic reproduction. There are historical cases of childless individuals who have craved fame as compensation for not being able to reproduce, such as Elizabeth I, who took great pains to ensure that her official portrait followed strict guidelines, drawing heavily on imagery associated with the Virgin Mary, or even John Lord Lumley, an early art collector of no note until all three of his children died, and he set about creating his own legend accordingly.[36] Again, I must emphasize that these are isolated cases. A thorough investigation would be of considerable interest.

Symbolic immortality

One of the features of the history of fame, as Braudy notes, is its apparent inverse relationship with the concept of the afterlife in any given culture. The societies of Ancient Egypt and Rome had gods but their idea of an afterlife was not strong. Reincarnation was popular, but the prospect of returning as a dung beetle has limited appeal compared with the Christian image of eternal salvation. Therefore it is not surprising to find the desire for fame flourishing in these earlier cultures, while it was certainly less popular during Medieval times when the Church had such a strong influence on Western society. More recently, the decline of religious faith in the West is in sharp contrast with the meteoric rise of celebrity culture.

There is a long literary tradition of presenting fame as immortality, from Virgil ('I too may... fly in victory on the lips of men') through to the lyrics of Irene Cara's song: 'Fame! I want to live forever!' Horace wrote that 'a great part of me will live beyond death', and Ovid echoed the sentiment. Later on,

Dante's contemporary Petrarch wrote of 'another life' that could be gained through fame. By the eighteenth century, with the decline in importance attached to the afterlife, the clamour for fame in one's lifetime was so loud that theologians took it as evidence for the existence of the immortal soul – even though it would seem to imply precisely the opposite.

Being famous for eternity is one thing: what about the instant fame of the moment? It appears that, as history unfolds, technological development has given us an increasing number of ways that we can achieve immortality – words, pictures, records, video. It is worth considering the origins of these technologies, because historically we can see that, intentionally or not, they have always been treated as forms of reproduction of the self. The reproduction of the human face in visual art, for instance, has been a source of controversy over the last two millennia. In Roman times, the appearance of the emperor's face on coins and sculptured busts of famous individuals were the earliest attempts to capture the human form. An important honour in Rome was the *ius imaginis* – the right to have one's face preserved for ever.[37]

With the rise of the Church, however, there was increasing concern about the visualization of the human form. Reproduction is God's business, they argued, and only images of Jesus (and later the saints) were appropriate – hence the huge trade in icons in Eastern Europe in the first few centuries AD. Later on, such practices were outlawed by the 'iconoclasts' on grounds of blasphemy. Henry VIII's destruction of religious images in sixteenth-century Britain coincided with the rise of portraiture, promoted partly by Henry himself. Initially, the only reproductions of human faces had been engravings, but now portraits and illustrations became immensely popular. Not only were they a means of reproducing oneself, but the reproduction could be tailored to present your best side – hence Henry's, and later Elizabeth I's incessant interest in achieving complete control over their portraits, reflecting the later concern of celebrities and their publicity photos.

Photographs as replicators

The invention of the camera was a major step in the reproduction of self. Even more than a portrait, a photograph was an unarguable verification of an individual's existence. We can go further than that. Each time we are photographed, it could be argued, *we reproduce*. This may seem a rather far-fetched analogy, but this is partly because we have become so familiar with photography that we take it for granted; so many people in Western society own a camera, and we see so many photographs every day (it is almost impossible to avoid seeing at least one photographic image each day, from a billboard poster or a shop window) that it is hard to imagine life without them. Once again, it is necessary to adopt a strict historical perspective in order to appreciate the significance of photography in terms of human evolution.

This point was not lost on the early pioneers of photography, or on the social commentators of the time. Daguerre, the inventor of the photographic process, described it as 'a chemical and physical process which gives nature the ability to reproduce herself.' Meanwhile, the *Leipzig City Advertiser* of 1837, in the tradition of the early Church, denounced the reproduction of the human face in film as sacrilegious: 'The very desire to do so is blasphemy. Man is created in the image of God and God's image cannot be captured by any human machine.'[38] It was acceptable for an artist to attempt it 'in a moment of solemnity', but 'never by means of a mechanical aid' (overlooking the technicality that a paintbrush might be considered a mechanical aid).

Suddenly, it seemed, the possibility of replicating ourselves without biologically reproducing was becoming a possibility; given the limitations of the concept, it could be said that photography was the first step on the road to human cloning.

Television as a better replicator

Compared with the crude reproductive capability of daguerrotype portraits, the invention of the cine-camera was a huge step towards the perfect reproduction of the human form. Now the arguments around the validity of representation no longer applied; although the recording of one's voice and one's visual image are coded pieces of information, the reproductions are so lifelike that we have little option but to treat them as such. This phenomenon is described by postmodernists as *simulacrum* – 'a state of such near perfect replication that the difference between the original and the copy becomes almost impossible to spot'.[39]

With the advent of television, there were simulacra of human beings everywhere. The early film industry had already placed film stars in a compromising position (for example the Myrna Loy quote in Chapter 2 about being the property of the studio). Now the famous were becoming the property of the public. For half an hour you could have Tony Hancock in your living room – and not just a visual representation of Tony Hancock, either – a walking, talking, (almost) three-dimensional representation of him, which sufficiently convinces you that it *is* Tony Hancock that you interact with him as though he were *there*.[40]

Return to the scenario on the opening page of the book. Again, put yourself in the shoes of the famous female recording artist. Shortly after your harrowing experience with the paparazzi, you are summoned to the studio by your record company (from the Los Angeles apartment you now rent) who insist that your contract requires you to make a second LP. The company urges you to release a particular song as a single ahead of the LP's release to act as a 'trailer' for it and, more importantly, as an opportunity for a burst of publicity work.

Your single is released and your press office arranges over 100 interviews for you, although you soon whittle this down to around half, spaced over a fortnight. You are booked into a plush hotel for most of them, although some take place elsewhere (such as television studios). In the week prior to the release of your single, you are being replicated furiously. Dozens of newspapers and glossy, full-colour magazines carry photographs of you along with the interview (and occasionally to accompany a news item about the release of your single). The video, for a start, receives heavy 'rotation' on specialist TV channels and several plays on terrestrial TV. You appear on a number of television shows to perform the song, and give a number of interviews. To gain maximum mileage out of you, a couple of shows, such as Saturday morning kids' TV, manage to persuade you to take part in some lowbrow slapstick comedy. The record is on the playlist at BBC radio and most commercial stations. Then the single is released, sells tens of thousands of copies, and provokes another week or two of saturation media coverage.

Think: each time someone plays your record, every time a radio is switched on while your song is being played, has you stroll into their living room via the television set, you are *there*.

How many appearances have *you* made in a week? Probably hundreds of thousands of copies of *you* are floating around Great Britain (not to mention the rest of the world, where you will replicate yourself at a later date).

No wonder so many of us want to be famous.

Conclusion

In this chapter, the historical perspective has been broadened to include an evolutionary perspective as well. The focus in general has been on the desire to be famous, which is clearly something that obsesses many of us, occasionally to a dangerous degree. I have considered arguments that there may indeed be something special about the 'special people' we celebrate – that the answer may lie in their personality or even in their genes. Alternatively I have considered social constructionist explanations for fame's appeal and the reproduction of seductive discourses through the media. However these approaches seem inadequate to account fully for the long-standing and desperate desire for fame. My main argument in this chapter is that technological developments over time have enabled us to reproduce ourselves in a way that mimics the replication of DNA. I have argued that the progressive invention of better and better replicating devices, culminating in television and video, have opened up opportunities for individuals to reproduce themselves on a phenomenal scale, thus providing an evolutionary rationale for the obsessive pursuit of fame (albeit at a cultural, rather than biological, level).

Chapter 4
Fame and the 'general public'

When we encounter celebrities in real life, our immediate sensation is often one of intense familiarity. We are certain we know that person from somewhere, and a split-second later we feel rather foolish when we realize it is someone we have never spoken to, who is ignorant of our individual existence, yet seems as familiar as a close neighbour or a long-lost friend.

Having stressed the importance of television for its replicatory potential, it seems reasonable to examine ways in which those replications of human beings are then treated by viewers. Once again, in order to appreciate the significance of television, film and video we need to ignore the recent past, and don the shoes of a time traveller from centuries past, walking into a modern living room and seeing people in a box, walking and talking in perfect reproduction. In this chapter I shall review the most important research conducted so far on the psychological effects of television, ranging from its social influence to the fantasy/reality debate and the phenomenon of parasocial interaction.[1]

Compare the way we watch people on television, particularly actors in dramas, with the way we watch the people around us in our daily life. The screen directs our visual attention towards the face, often in vivid detail (modern American soaps, such as the Sky series *Days of Our Lives*, have an unnerving penchant for zooming in on characters' faces at dramatic moments, eventually coming so close that their facial features alone fill the entire screen). Unless we combine television watching with another activity that requires a lot of visual contact (reading, perhaps) we are obliged to spend many minutes, eventually hours, observing the details of characters from all angles. We get to recognize them the moment they appear on screen – particularly if, in the case of soaps, they reappear night after night.

Television and psychology

It seems surprising that mainstream psychologists have said relatively little about television, given the prominent part it has played in the second half of the twentieth century. It may be that it has crept up on us so stealthily, and so insidiously, that we have barely had time to take stock of its importance before sending researchers into the field to study it. It may also be that it poses problems for essentialist psychology by being a cultural innovation, and so any 'effects' that it might cause are likely to have a cultural rather than a biological basis. As a result, the bulk of research into psychology and television has been carried out, not by psychologists, but by media and communications researchers.

Nevertheless, it was clear when radio first gained mass popularity before the Second World War that this type of mass communication would exert a range of cognitive effects. An early American study of the psychology of radio reported on a number of studies investigating its impact, including some experimental work on the perception of speech in the absence of a speaker.[2] The authors were deeply concerned about the use of radio to spread propaganda, such as political extremism; some justification was given to their views when, three years later, an extraordinary event took place. Early one evening, what seemed to be a dance programme was interrupted by a mock news report in which, it was disclosed, a meteor had landed in New Jersey and eyewitness reports spoke of Martians slaughtering hapless passers-by with deadly ray guns. It was nothing more than a dramatization of H.G. Wells' *War of the Worlds*, but it created panic throughout the country, with distressed listeners jamming phone lines, traffic grinding to a halt, and at least one listener allegedly attempting suicide.

This extreme reaction from a large section of the radio audience to a work of fiction seems implausible at the end of the twentieth century, and yet the really incredible fact is that we have become such sophisticated media consumers in so comparatively short a time. The same is true of television. Even programmes made as recently as the early 1980s seem, by the end of the century, remarkably dated in production techniques, dialogue and presentation. The recent cult revival of science fiction series from the 1960s, such as *Lost in Space* and *Doctor Who*, is a case in point. And yet, however clever we may appear today, it is surely our constant obsession with the medium over the last 50 years that has forced it – and us – to make such rapid progress.

The earliest studies of psychology and television were chiefly concerned with its impact on the psychological development of children.[3] Some of the topics under investigation seem rather quaint today: would TV damage children's eyesight? What was a safe distance to sit from the screen? Would children skip their homework to stare at the box all evening? What would the effect be on levels of literacy? There was a general fear that television might stunt children's social development, by keeping them indoors rather than engaging in social interaction outside the home (ironically, today, the locus of concern is reversed). Increasingly the research questions switched to television's influence on children's behaviour away from the screen, particularly aggressive behaviour in the playground. The role of the mass media in the apparent rise in violent crime has been a popular topic of investigation in the last 30 years, largely as a result of the increasing availability of violent videos.[4]

Most research in the area now concedes that television exerts important influences on our psychological lives, but what do we retain from our viewing? It certainly seems to be the case that television viewers recall more visual than verbal information; recall of TV news, for instance, is generally poor for semantic information,[5] but even semantic recall may be boosted by vivid visual imagery.[6] This may be partly a function of viewing habit: in one study by George Comstock and colleagues, it was found that for many viewers, watching television is very much a secondary activity – other activities take priority, even if the set is continually switched on.[7] Indeed, this may account for the remarkable statistic that the average American adult spends more time watching television than any other activity apart from working and sleeping![8] This suggests that television's effect is largely subliminal: the images seep into our subconscious even when we are not fully paying attention.

One of the problems of much of the psychological research into television is that the focus is still directed towards its perceived negative features (as I suggested earlier, psychological research has a tendency to be *problem*-driven). A case in point is John Condry's *The Psychology of Television*,[9] whose title might lead one to expect the definitive work in the field, but which devotes much of its attention to the supposed causal relationship between television and aggression, or more specifically, violence. Kubey and Csikszentmihalyi's *Television and the Quality of Life: How Viewing Shapes Everyday Experience*,[10] the work of two highly respected and much-published American psychologists, starts promisingly but soon descends into a labyrinth of figures and charts demonstrating the effect watching television has on attention and arousal, and how much it drains something called 'psychic energy'. A whole chapter is devoted to the physiological effects of 'heavy' viewing. The term 'reality' is used to denote anything *except* the experience of television; humans are reduced to passive processors of information, most of it undesirable and vulgar. Children are particularly at risk: 'The child is condemned to develop a viewing habit, the choices determined by the poverty of the environment.'[11] Television is a black hole into which people pour their consciousness, rejecting 'serious cultural fare' and generally wasting their valuable time. The wheel has come full circle from those early papers on the effects of television; now it is our brains, not our eyes, that are in danger of being irreparably damaged by the box.[12]

Cross-cultural research

The problem of external validity (how far can we apply laboratory-based findings to 'real life'?) is a constant concern for those conducting (or interpreting) experimental research in psychology, and so perhaps the most interesting work is that conducted on the impact of television on societies who received television at a relatively late stage in global terms. A special issue of the *Journal of Cross-Cultural Psychology* in September 1985 carried a number of reports from parts of northern Canada where television had not been widely introduced until the 1970s, thus providing the perfect opportunity for what scientists call 'natural experiments'.[13]

The findings of these studies indicate that some of the original concerns of television researchers were quite valid. Television did indeed act as a displacement activity, especially among older adults, and community events suffered as a result of television's arrival.[14] Also, children's reading acquisition suffered according to the amount of television they watched, and playground aggression increased in the areas which began to receive television. There was an added problem in that increased exposure to Western culture was having negative effects upon viewers' perception of their own traditional culture (although this was partly assuaged with the development of local television networks).

One study of a mixed sample of viewers from the Far East, Britain and the United States found that across cultures, people treated television as a 'significant other' – in other words, they absorbed the same types of information in their relationship with people on the screen as they did with actual human beings.[15] An earlier study argued that, in serving this purpose, television has taken on the functions of the village community of earlier years.[16] When television was first introduced into a Native Canadian community with a strong shamanic tradition, there was no doubt that television was a straightforward updating of traditional ways of educating and entertaining people:

> This was the shaman's conjuring tent in which a seance could be held with dead people, spirits, or people living some distance away, and in which news from all over the world could be obtained, even knowledge of the future or of hidden things. Indeed, the Cree word for this tent was identified as the best word that could serve as a translation for the English word 'television'.[17]

Reality monitoring and 'tele-literacy'

Perhaps the most important literature on television and psychology concerns viewers' interpretations of 'reality'. Communications researchers Shapiro and McDonald[18] contrast two basic types of reality: physical reality (what is really there) and representational reality (it appears to be there but isn't). Pre-school children may believe that television characters are little people inside the set itself, even being lowered down by a rope.[19] Identifying children's interpretation of 'reality' is, however, made difficult if we try to impose adult logic on their explanations, such as the idea that children will 'transfer' what they see on television to their everyday social interaction.[20] There is no reason to suppose that children see television as a 'representation' of reality any more than as a parallel universe, a container housing particularly entertaining varieties of domestic pet, or a book that moves. A child needs a significant amount of knowledge about the world in order to see television as representational in the first place.[21]

In one series of studies, communications researchers Byron Reeves and Clifford Nass claim to have demonstrated that people react to television as though it were physical reality.[22] They refer to this as the 'media equation', suggesting that the users of television and computers equate perceived reality with physical reality, thereby challenging 'the cherished assumption that words and pictures in media are *symbolic representations* of things that are not actually present'.[23] Their approach has been to conduct experimental studies of human interaction with media in precisely the same way that psychologists have studied human interaction with other humans. By producing a similar set of results, Reeves and Nass claim that mediated communication is no different from interpersonal communication.

This interpretation has high face validity – it sounds plausible. But again we are faced with the problem of generalizing on the basis of artificial laboratory studies. For example, one study investigated brain activity while subjects watched a sausage rolling towards them on a television screen. Sure enough, attention increased as the sausage rolled closer; but to infer from this that we are reacting as though a *real* sausage was heading for our face stretches credulity. To generalize from this finding, and suggest that people interact with television on an everyday basis the way they interact with images on the screens in the laboratory, is to overlook the important point that, in a natural setting, television is rarely watched with the intensity of an experimental subject, and the care the researchers took to ensure that viewing was the 'primary activity' may have damaged the ecological validity of the research.

An alternative suggestion is that we learn to 'read' television both ontologically (as children develop) and chronologically (as the medium evolves over time). This process has been described as *tele-literacy*.[24] What this means is that, rather than learning to perceive television as a direct, one-to-one representational system, we learn to identify its formal characteristics. One early example of this is children learning how to distinguish animated characters from human ones. Later on, we learn how to distinguish between a fictional programme and documentary programmes (including news bulletins). Rather than seeing the former as 'fantasy' and the latter as 'reality' – although this is the distinction adults try to encourage – it is probably the case that children are simply learning to identify different types of broadcasting convention, such as the style of presentation and camera-work.[25]

Three levels of representation have been identified that children learn to distinguish: one-to-one representation (an image of a car moving along a road); media conventions (such as a camera zoom or change of angle); and general symbolism (such as the representational function of a set of traffic lights). Older children begin to base their reality judgments at the last level – in other words, they are beginning to transfer ideas from real life and to use these to rationalize what they see on television.[26] Maire Messenger Davies explored this in the context of the US children's show *Sesame Street*. While even the younger children were able to judge the character Big Bird as unreal, the older children were able to base reality judgments on plausibility. For example, each time one character attempted to play the piano he was interrupted by the doorbell. This was seen as a clear fictional device.[27] Clearly we have come a long way from those horrified radio listeners in 1938.

Identification with people on the screen

Although we do seem to be pretty good at differentiating between styles of media presentation, the influence of the 'media equation' may be rather more subtle than the experimental evidence might suggest. As discussed at the end of Chapter 3, television is an excellent replicator for a human individual. Indeed, Reeves and Nass have carried out some studies which allow children to talk about television characters, and discovered that they use precisely the same personality attributes as they would to describe real people, even when the characters were animations.

The significance of seeing real people projected on to a screen has not been lost on film researchers. Much of the early work on the way viewers respond to film stars was rooted in the psychoanalytic tradition, and described their affiliation in terms of 'identification' – whether or not we empathize with a character, or construe them as 'hostile', or whatever. This rather abstract symbolic way of describing what happens when we are watching people on screen is clearly insufficient to capture the rich interactivity that we engage in.

The original assumptions of 'identification' with film stars have since been challenged.[28] One film researcher approached the readers of a women's weekly magazine and asked them to reminisce about their favourite Hollywood stars from the 1940s and 50s. The responses indicated that far more than mere 'identification' was taking place. Four typical reactions were produced. The first was to idealize the star (one respondent described Rita Hayworth as 'the most perfect woman I had ever seen'); another was to adopt the star as a role model (of Betty Grable, 'how could a young girl not want to look like that?'); a third response was to draw inspiration from their characters (such as Bette Davis who 'quelled her leading men with a raised eyebrow and sneer'); and finally there was an escapist response ('I was no longer in my seat'). As a result of these reactions, the respondents had deliberately modelled their appearance and behaviour on their idols, in their application of make-up, choice of clothes and hairstyles, and even pretended to be the stars in certain social situations.

Evidently, this 'carryover' effect from screen to everyday interaction suggests something more profound than simple empathy; it is as though the stars were performing the role of a close friend. Now that the stars are able to appear in our homes, through television, we might expect to form many close friendships.

Parasocial interaction

If identification is not a sufficiently strong term to describe what happens when we interact with a person appearing on screen, what might be a more suitable alternative? The most useful research on television viewing, for the purposes of this book, comes from media and communication researchers, who have gone on to suggest that we actually form *relationships* with the people on screen. This research recognizes that television viewing is qualitatively different from watching a film in a cinema – programming conventions are one important difference, as is the everyday, 'heavy' use of the medium, and the casual manner in which we watch. 'While identification with texts and characters may explain viewing of a specific program, it seldom explains all viewing (especially when people watch even though "there's nothing on").'[29]

The term 'para-social interaction' was coined in an article in the journal *Psychiatry* back in the 1950s.[30] The authors argued that media consumers form relationships with media characters, albeit unilateral relationships, that affect us in ways that resemble any other relationship with a person. 'They [the viewers] "know" such a persona in somewhat the same way they know their chosen friends; through direct observation and interpretation of his appearance, his gestures and voice, his conversation and conduct in a variety of situations.'[31] Since then, the term 'para-social interaction' has formed part of what is commonly referred to as the 'uses and gratifications' approach to mass communication.

The emergence of radio as a form of mass communication had already paved the way for the kind of para-social interaction that television engaged viewers in after the war. Paddy Scannell, who has extensively researched the social impact of radio in its early years, writes that initially, 'broadcasters thought of themselves as "uninvited guests" in the family living room.'[32] This high degree of realization of the public's relationship with the media is a stark contrast to the blasé attitude of modern celebrities! It has much to do with radio's novelty at the time, and early broadcasting techniques, such as the development of the 'fireside' style of simulated intimacy in the voice, can be attributed to broadcasters' sensitivity to their function.

The formation of parasocial relationships

The first time we encounter a media persona, we make the same set of judgments as we make the first time we encounter a real human being. Do we like the look of them? Do we share any common interests or characteristics (for example, culture, gender)? Do they behave in a manner that pleases us? Are we sexually attracted to them, even? (In the case of pornography, the parasocial equivalent of prostitution, this may be our sole criterion of assessment.) Most importantly of all, would we like to meet them again?

Up to this point, all of these features indicate that some form of social interaction is taking place. But when does an interaction become a relationship? As Rubin and McHugh suggest,[33] a relationship is formed when the interaction continues after the set is turned off; if the initial encounter has been satisfying, the viewer will re-engage in the interaction, and an ongoing relationship will develop. It has even been claimed that viewers often try to engage television people verbally, for instance, by responding to a newsreader's greeting.[34] Indeed, one of the items on the PSI (parasocial interaction) scale devised by Rubin, Perse and Powell asks respondents to what extent they agree with the statement 'I sometimes make remarks to my favorite television performer during the program'.[35] This is almost certainly an aspect of local culture; it would be interesting to compare these (North American) findings with those of, say, a British sample.[36]

There is some research that suggests that many of the features of parasocial relationships are similar to those of ordinary relationships. One (very obvious) example is that we tend to use the same cues for evaluating TV people positively as we do for real people – attractiveness, shared values, attitudes, background and communicative styles.[37] One researcher[38] has gone as far as to say that the experience of being in a parasocial relationship is the same as the experience of being in a real relationship. Laura Leets and colleagues[39] have identified three ways in which parasocial relationships may develop along similar lines to real relationships: firstly, through a process of 'uncertainty reduction' (we like people the more we get to know them and we can predict their behaviour); secondly, we each evaluate our parasocial relations using our unique set of personal constructs[40] in the same way as we evaluate our real relationships; and thirdly, drawing on social exchange theory, we receive the same 'costs' and 'rewards' from parasocial exchanges as we do from real ones.

It seems likely that the relationships we form with fictional characters – particularly those appearing in soap operas – are different from those we form with 'real' people on television, such as television personalities, although no major studies of such a distinction have yet been published. However, I have recently obtained some interview data which suggest that the distinction between soap characters and real-life celebrities may be considerably blurred, certainly from the perspective of 'response'. Indeed there are numerous reports of soap characters being treated by the general public as though 'in character'. For example, when a character experiences misfortune in a story line, television companies are often besieged with flowers and letters from viewers. It is reported that, 'during the first five years of his appearance in the popular series *Marcus Welby M.D.*, actor Robert Young received over a quarter of a million letters from viewers, mostly asking for medical advice.'[41] It may be that the conventions of soap opera (its large proportion of airtime, its regularity of exposure, and the naturalism of its storylines) produce the strongest parasocial interaction of all.

The most obvious criticism of parasocial interaction studies, however, is that they tend to under-estimate the importance of user control over technological devices. For example, if someone we dislike appears on our television, we can switch off the set and refuse to enter into a relationship. By giving the user such control over parasocial interaction, it lends the relationships we form an aura of escapism; as Cohen and Metzger put it, 'television represents the perfect guest – one who comes and leaves at our whim.'[42] However, for young children the issue of user control is not so relevant, and it may be that future research on the formation of parasocial relationships should be directed at this viewing population.[43]

Substitute relationships?

Some researchers[44] suggest that socially isolated individuals may use television to satisfy their need for actual relationships, and some of the cross-cultural research into television viewing behaviour suggests that, especially for women (many of their sample were heavy mid-afternoon soap-opera viewers), parasocial interaction may fill important gaps in social life. Other work suggests that there is a positive correlation between the formation of parasocial relationships and the amount of television viewed.[45]

The advantages of parasocial relationships over real ones may be those relating to user control; a parasocial partner does not interact with *you*, does not let you down, and therefore you have a degree of power in a parasocial relationship. Your partner can contain all manner of fantasy attributes that may put real potential partners in the shade. Parasocial interaction can provide you with the ideal partner; not only a living being with all the appropriate physical attributes, but also someone whose every move is publicly scrutinized. The feeling that we know 'the real person' behind the celebrity through the exposure of the media makes us feel also that we are under no illusions. As a fan of the British actor Colin Firth says: 'You don't know someone who you meet at a party until you get to know them...I know as much about Colin Firth as I did my last boyfriend when I started going out with him.'[46]

Perhaps the most blatant use of parasocial interaction as a substitute for real relationships is in the use of pornography. Indeed, the phenomenal success of the pornography industry may be all the evidence we need to demonstrate the psychological importance of parasocial interaction. Masturbation with the aid of pornography is an extraordinary psychological phenomenon, far beyond the explanatory scope of evolutionary theory, but the small amount of psychological research into responses to 'erotica' largely consists of laboratory-based experiments that tell us little about the real-life *use* of pornography.[47]

Parasocial interaction in groups

When more than one person engages in parasocial interaction, does this weaken the formation of parasocial relationships? Cross-cultural research[48] suggests that men rather than women tend to watch television in small groups (though this may be an idiosyncrasy of their sample rather than a valid gender preference) – for example, a group of men gathering to watch a football match. The same study also suggested that the type of programme preferred by men is less likely to lead to meaningful parasocial interaction (there is only so much interaction one can have with 22 footballers in 90 minutes!). However, with patterns of television viewing continually changing, the factor of gender is one which fluctuates with cultural preferences. Nevertheless, it has been argued that women are better at forming close relationships with fictional characters (hence the apparently higher preference for soap operas among female viewers) and what to a masculine perspective seems 'over-involvement' does not preclude female viewers from being able to adopt a 'critical distance'.[49] This may prove an interesting line of inquiry in future research in this area.

There are good reasons to suggest that not only what we watch, but who we watch it with, are important considerations for parasocial interaction. Some research has suggested that watching television or films in groups can have quite a dramatic effect on emotional behaviour. For example, in one study it was found that groups of teenagers watching graphic scenes in horror movies reacted with laughter rather than squirming or recoiling in disgust as would be expected.[50] This may be attributed to the coping strategies of disbelief which viewers sometimes employ in the cinema, especially when the content of a film is likely to be disagreeable. Work with children suggests that the ability to suspend disbelief for 'frightening' material starts as early as age four.[51] This can of course be contrasted with the high degree of emotional identification viewers engage in where films or programmes have a romantic content, where the shedding of tears is far from uncommon, even in highly public settings such as a cinema. Likewise, comedy programmes and films may also produce an exaggerated response when viewed in groups,[52] suggesting that humour relies heavily on social context for its effect, rather than individual rational response.

Furthermore, as suggested earlier, an important characteristic of any relationship is that it continues in the absence of the other person. An important function parasocial relationships serve is as conversational material in group settings. Soap operas are a prime example of this function (as, to a lesser extent, is sport). The relationships viewers form with soap characters persist well beyond the daily half-hour of interaction, since they inform the positions held in conversation with fellow viewers, where the soap characters – their behaviour, their perceived motives, their futures – are discussed as though they were real acquaintances. Because of their naturalistic setting, and the regularity of our exposure to the characters, soap operas probably represent the most fertile ground for future research into parasocial interaction.

'Public access' media

So far I have discussed the general public's relationship with the media as though it were entirely passive: we are just consumers, our most meaningful experiences are 'parasocial' ones, and so on. This may have been true in the immediate post-war period, when television first made its appearance in our homes, but it was not long before the general public started being invited across the great divide between public space and media space, to take part in television shows, not just as an invisible studio audience, but as the starring role.

This type of show has become known as 'public access television', and has become so popular that it occupies a large portion of programming time. For example, on 19 June 1998 (a random date – it just happens to coincide with writing this chapter) there were 19 programmes on the five British terrestrial channels alone which could be described as public access shows, and this during an exceptionally heavy day of live sporting action (two World Cup matches, a test match, Royal Ascot and pre-Wimbledon warm-up tennis from Eastbourne).

The 19 programmes could be classified as:

- 'Talk' shows – *Kilroy, Vanessa, The Oprah Winfrey Show*, and so on;
- Game shows – *Countdown, House Hunters*, and so on;
- Programmes with public access features, for example, *Blue Peter*;
- Programmes with visible audience participation, for example, *TFI Friday*.

Public access television has its origins, like so many other television phenomena, in radio broadcasting. In the 1930s, the BBC in Manchester began broadcasting programmes which involved a celebrity interviewing members of the public about their daily activities, in an effort to give local radio a distinct regional flavour. In the 1940s, the need to maintain national morale resulted in similar shows being broadcast throughout Britain, designed to demonstrate to listeners the nationwide efforts and spirit of people during wartime. After the war, the general public became even more involved in the broadcasts in shows such as *Have A Go!*, which included extensive interviews with 'ordinary working-class' members of the public.[53]

Parasocial interaction clearly takes on a different aspect when the interaction is with fellow members of the general public rather than established stars. We appreciate that members of the public are unlikely to reappear on television, and that it may not be worth forming a parasocial relationship with them. As a result, we tend to be rather scathing about the general public on television (unless we know them already). We respond by saying: 'Who do they think they are, occupying this airtime?' or 'What has *she* done to deserve a TV appearance rather than me?'

I have painted here what may be a peculiarly cynical British response to public appearances on television. In the United States the response would appear to be quite different. In a study by Patricia Priest[54] a number of 'talk show' participants were interviewed about their experiences during, and after, the broadcast. There was a general feeling among the participants that they had 'gained access to' what Priest describes as 'a sacred cultural space' or 'inner sanctum' in which dwell all the 'deities' with whom people have established parasocial relationships from the other side of the TV screen. As if to confirm the semi-religious experience afforded to those people lucky enough to cross the boundary to this inner sanctum, one participant claimed that, when shopping the following day, he encountered a couple of strangers who 'stopped like they seen God'.

Many of Priest's participants spoke of the 'celebrity' status they had acquired, however briefly, in the period after the show had been aired. One of the most interesting aspects of the study was that, whatever people had *said* on the show, it seemed to take second berth to the simple fact that they *appeared* on it. One man had appeared on *Donahue* to break the news that, not only was he HIV positive, but in the three weeks after learning of this diagnosis, he had worked for an escort service having unprotected sex with several clients. He expected to be lynched by the viewing public after receiving a roasting from the studio audience, and yet the responses were almost wholly positive. A woman who had appeared on television discussing her life as a trans-sexual lesbian was somewhat disappointed when members of the public greeted her and simply glossed over the subject she had discussed.

Good news perhaps, for those who feel they have gone over the top in their contributions; not so good news for those who use public access television as a cathartic outlet, or an opportunity to get a close secret off their chests. Here, research with people who have unwittingly been part of television coverage following tragic incidents would be interesting.

The making of Maureen

Recent trends in programme-making have introduced a new style of interaction with the people we see on television. A currently popular genre of programme has been identified as a 'fly-on-the-wall' (FOW) documentary. A typical FOW selects a theme, usually a profession, and spends the initial programme introducing a number of characters, whose exploits are documented for several weeks. For example, a series about medical school may focus on four students, and each episode features the students doing all the things a 'typical' medical student would be expected to do (and more besides!). The four students would be selected probably through a screening process beforehand (carried out via the medical school itself), so they would fit criteria that made them interesting to the general public (for example, viewers would be able to sympathize with student A, would be irritated by student B, and so on). By the second or third week of the series, the characters would be sufficiently developed for viewers to be intensely interested in their exploits. As viewers became more familiar with this style of programme they were more likely to form parasocial relationships with the characters from the first episode, and soon it became evident that certain characters had 'star quality', or vast audience appeal. Perhaps the most striking example of such a character to date is Maureen Reece, the 'star' of the BBC series *Driving School*.

Driving School was a FOW featuring a number of driving instructors and a number of regular learners whom the instructors were teaching. The format was similar to other FOWs featuring students in that viewers would follow the series to its conclusion to see whether or not the students would qualify. Among the regular learners selected to appear on the series was a woman from Bristol called Maureen Reece, whose attempts to drive had spanned several years and seven failed tests. Footage of her long-suffering husband coaching her frantically from the passenger seat while she weaved in and out of traffic lanes and mounted pavements provided the BBC with outstanding entertainment. After the first two shows it was clear that it was Maureen's story that would capture the imagination of the viewing public; promotional trailers for the show featured her antics prominently, and before long Maureen (she is rarely referred to by her surname) was well-known enough to be the subject of newspaper stories and features on other television programmes. By the final episode in the series she was finally ready to take another test, and 12 million viewers watched as she finally passed in a car fitted with an automatic gearbox.

The show's conclusion did not signal the end of Maureen Reece's fame. She appeared on numerous television and radio shows, including the draw for the National Lottery and, somewhat controversially, *This Is Your Life* – a biographical programme which is traditionally a showcase only for major celebrities near the end of a long career. Like many other celebrities, she has described her own personal highlight as meeting the Queen (at a Royal Variety Show performance). In the sacred space that is the British television world, there are many doors to pass through, and the Queen inhabits the room behind the very last door. Maureen finally reached that last room.

What are we to make of the Maureen Reece story? Although she was, effectively, a media creation, the media do not operate in a vacuum; an astute public-response procedure informs their decisions about which programmes and celebrities are likely to be popular and successful, and it was clear from early in the *Driving School* campaign that Maureen had a tragi-comic allure and a lack of affectation that viewers might warm to. To say that viewers 'identified' with Maureen is, once again, not enough; maybe she represents the next-door neighbour, or the woman you see regularly in the bus queue or at the supermarket checkout – someone *so* ordinary that a real relationship might be a distinct possibility. All the same, the cultural connotations of celebrities' 'ordinariness' may be more politicized than we like to think.[55]

Fly-on-the-wall celebrities did not stop with Maureen. Shortly afterwards a BBC camera crew joined an ocean liner on a cruise (programme: *The Cruise*) and featured a cabaret singer who appeared to have missed her opportunity to find fame and fortune. But as a result of *The Cruise*'s popularity, Jane McDonald recorded an album which later entered the UK charts at number one. Another FOW success were two trainee veterinary surgeons (*Vets in Practice*) who met during the making of the show and eventually got married – in a special television show attracting over 10 million viewers.

How long can this trend continue? The television viewing world is a bottomless pit of potential celebrities, but the novelty value must soon wear off. Or will it? Perhaps the democratization of fame is still not complete.

Conclusion

If this chapter seems to be less about fame than about the technological experiences of the general population, that is because the two have, in the twentieth century, become increasingly intertwined. The experience of visiting the cinema, and 'identifying' with your favourite film star, has evolved, through television, into a complex network of interrelationships in which we, as viewers, have an increasing ability to share the sacred space of the media with our idols. Furthermore, the high visibility of the general public in the media has led to the creation of celebrities who are otherwise unremarkable members of the public who have been turned into stars by the activities of the television camera. The man you can see from your window anonymously hoeing his garden may be presenting the National Lottery draw in a year's time.

In such a cultural climate the meaning of fame changes again: far from the traditional fame in recognition of great deeds, today 'celebrity' has taken on an air of vulgarity. If the next-door neighbour can become a star for no particular reason, then maybe fame is not worth having. Rather than lessening our desire for fame, however, such cultural shifts may simply reinforce our need to appear 'special', and reap the right sort of recognition. But if fame is essentially an unprincipled, amoral deity, how can we guarantee that this will happen? The problem of reconciling the arbitrary nature of fame with the feeling of personal worth is the topic of the next chapter.

Chapter 5
Identity crises: the perils of 'authenticity'

'The celebrity... is the public representation of individuality in contemporary culture', writes the cultural critic David Marshall.[1] For Marshall, the phenomenon of celebrity is contemporaneous with the emergence of psychology as a discipline. Both are symbol systems, he argues, through which capitalism retains its hold on society, by reducing all human activity to private 'personalities' and the inner life of the individual.[2] In these next two chapters, however, I intend to shift attention away from the perspective of symbolism (or semiotics) towards the social, and indeed private, *experience* of fame.

While acknowledging the fact that the 'psychologizing' of society may have deeply conservative roots,[3] it seems to me of little intellectual value simply to ignore the experiences of individuals, and since the individual, as explained in Chapter 2, has come to occupy such a central position in Western culture, it is clearly a very meaningful perspective from which to explore the phenomenon of fame. At the same time, it is impossible to ignore the cultural and historical nature of celebrity, since the same issues are of crucial importance when considering the nature of the private 'self'. And it is here that a great deal of the existing psychological literature is relevant to the current project.

'The self' in psychology

In modern Western culture, it might seem that the individual self is such a taken-for-granted reality that its origins require little discussion. However, there has been an awareness in recent years of just how context-bound our notion of 'self' is, and a realization that many of the concepts surrounding self and individuality that we have so long regarded as universal and essential to human nature may simply be cultural artefacts of our present historical situation.

One example of the way the modern self has emerged is in the proliferation of English expressions relating to putative cognitive processes originating in the self: selfish, self-consciousness, self-awareness, self-esteem, self-worth, self-knowledge and self-interest, just to name a handful. The American psychologist Kurt Danziger has traced the origin of some of these terms to the seventeenth century, and a move away from the idea of human beings as participants in a 'cosmic order' to a separation of 'world' and self. Prior to this point, the self was often portrayed in opposition to God, as intrinsically sinful.[4]

However, the empiricist philosophers of the time decried the existence of the self as any meaningful entity, since it was not open to scientific investigation (that is, measurement). With the arrival of psychology as a science, the self was ignored again, behaviourists preferring to see the individual mind as a 'black box' whose contents were too elusive and mysterious to be worthy of study. The 'cognitive revolution' of the post-war period eventually turned the spotlight back on the processing qualities of the individual mind, this time using computational metaphors and analogies.

Out of this field emerged what has become known as 'social cognition' – the study of social interaction from the perspective of the individual mind. This branch of psychology specialized in the development of psychometric instruments for measuring characteristics of the private self: measures of self-esteem, self-discrepancy, self-consciousness, and so on. At the same time, humanist psychologists such as Carl Rogers and Abraham Maslow rediscovered the self as the central focus of investigation, mainly from a self-improvement perspective of the kind pioneered by Benjamin Franklin.

Meanwhile, there was a parallel development in the research of social psychologists and anthropologists who queried many of the assumptions that social cognitive psychologists were making about the nature of 'the self'. The idea of the self as a singular, internal characteristic of private individuals was, they argued, restricted to industrialized Western society. In an oft-quoted passage, the anthropologist Clifford Geertz has written: 'The Western conception of the person as a bounded, unique, more or less integrated motivational and cognitive universe ... [is] a rather peculiar idea within the context of the world's cultures.'[5]

Geertz was basing his argument largely on his work in societies such as Java and Bali, where he found that people used quite different terms to describe their individual existence, terms which linked them inextricably with social groups, such as kinship networks. Other studies have traced the development of the individuated self as occurring simultaneously with the growth of capitalism in the eighteenth and nineteenth centuries.[6] Indeed, it is now clear that psychology as a discipline emerged initially as a property of Western industrialism, through the conceptualization of the individual worker as a component in a machine, or the shell-shocked soldier as a vital weak link in a military unit. The creation of instruments to study and regulate individual citizens arose as a means of social control, and the application of such measures in a medical and scientific context has brought about new questions of ethics and power relations.[7]

From a historical perspective, it is not enough to see the individuated self as a product merely of capitalist society. As the history of fame outlined in Chapter 2 demonstrates, notions of selfhood have changed constantly since the birth of civilization as a result of cultural change and language development. One of the most important factors influencing the concept of self has been urbanization – first with the city-state of Rome, and later with the population explosion of the Middle Ages. The creation of private dwellings in cities may both symbolize and produce individualism, particularly in the wealthier sections of society. At all levels, changes in the internal organization of houses brought about different notions of privacy and selfhood.[8]

Another important influence on the Western self was the growth of Christianity, which, as I have stated earlier, had such a profound effect on pre-Renaissance Europe. Unlike ancient religions, Christianity promised salvation to even the humblest citizen through a one-to-one relationship with God established through prayer (a parasocial interaction of a different kind?). Although the notion of a soul or spirit was not new, the Christian concept of the soul as a 'real self' to be nourished by the individual in preparation for eternity in Heaven brought about an individualizing of Western society which shaped its subsequent development.[9]

The wane of the Church's influence in the Renaissance period led to new ways of expressing the soul, or inner self. For example, Leo Braudy writes of the paintings of Holbein in which Thomas More and his family are pictured, for the first time in portraiture, each looking away from the artist so that s/he appears to be lost in private thought. The implication here is that each individual in the painting has his or her own internal world; like Alexander's heavenward gaze, this is another posture that we find echoed in many modern celebrity pictures (in which subjects are typically described as 'pensive'). Later, the notion of an internal self that was consistent across time was introduced by philosophers like Locke and Hobbes, followed by a rash of words to describe the self.

The American psychologist Kenneth Gergen[10] has further distinguished between the 'romanticist' notion of the self and the rationalist, or 'modernist' notion, where the true self becomes a solid, knowable entity, and personality is a demonstrable, measurable quality of an individual, cast in concrete by genetic inheritance. This latter view of the self underpins the work of the humanists, whose approach was dominated by the need for individuals to 'discover' their true essence through a voyage of 'self-discovery'.[11] A similar approach was adopted by Abraham Maslow,[11] who argued that humans strive to achieve 'self-actualization', the highest state of being in a hierarchy of 'needs', which is characterized by a number of personal qualities which are clearly specific to American culture.[12]

The Western concept of self is a major factor behind the rise of celebrity. For a start, the aggrandizement of the individual within such a society creates the conditions for a culture of celebrity to thrive. There is therefore no real need to characterize this as a *modern* concept of self, since, as Braudy's work shows, a similar concept underlay early aspirations to fame, particularly in Roman society. It may be that *urbanization*, rather than industrialization *per se*, is the single most important factor in the evolution of individualist culture. It must be remembered that, initially, Roman self-glory was reflected in the glory of the Roman state, and it was not until Augustus, Caligula, and others, that the specific individual took precedence. Moreover, this concept of self was restricted to the ruling classes.

Today, the study of 'the self' in psychology is pulled in three directions. Firstly, the social constructionist approach encourages psychologists to look beyond the individual self as an object of study to the ways in which self, or 'identity', is constructed in discourse.[13] Secondly, psychologists continue to write uncritically about 'the self', often when they use older approaches, such as Erikson's lifespan model, or Loevinger's 'ego development' theory, to inform research in areas such as adolescence or ageing.[14]

The third direction is somewhat problematic, since it blends a healthy cross-cultural perspective with a seemingly desperate attempt to measure something called 'self-construal'. What *is* self-construal? A number of researchers suggest that it is the way an individual views the self along various dimensions, which have been characterized as independent or interdependent,[15] individual or collective,[16] and allocentric or idiocentric.[17]

These studies argue that individuals in East Asian cultures construct an 'interdependent' sense of self, where individuals tend to define themselves in relation to social groups and strata, and strive towards harmony with others. Westerners, on the other hand, tend to have a more 'independent' sense of self, in which the individual describes himself or herself as though detached from the remainder of society (through concepts like self-sufficiency and autonomy).

One study[18] even suggests that *within* Western society, a similar contrast can be drawn between the 'self-construals' of men and those of women, with women defining themselves in relation to others, and men favouring a detachment of self. There is a wealth of evidence to support such a distinction – one example being a study in which men and women were asked to describe their lives using photographs of themselves: women included a significantly larger number of 'group' (for example, family) pictures, while men included more pictures of themselves alone.[19]

However, the use of the term 'self-construal' is problematic. Apart from it being a cumbersome term anyway, it seems to be over-simplistic (Cross and Madson do, admittedly, argue that they use it to avoid further complicating the literature, which is fair enough). For one thing, Cross and Madson describe the 'interdependent' self-construal (East Asian/female) as incorporating flexible representations of the self, such as a person being serious with parents but lighthearted with friends.[20] The 'independent' self-construal (Western/male), by contrast, allows for no such flexibility of representation. To apply this almost autistic state of social inflexibility to the majority of Western males is somewhat harsh. Furthermore, the argument that individuals may differ in their type of self-construal (in other words, it is possible to avoid enculturation) seems to contradict the very notion of 'interdependence'. How can one isolated individual possess an interdependent self-construal and not his or her peers? The idea of 'self-construal', I suspect, may be the wrong tree up which to bark.[21]

Elsewhere, postmodernist psychologists such as Kenneth Gergen have suggested that the individuated self is fast fragmenting into 'multiphrenia' through the influence of modern technology. This theory is worth considering in some detail because it ties in with some of the ideas considered in Chapters 3 and 4, notably the *replicating* power of television and other forms of mass communication. For Gergen, the ability to be in two places at once (for example, watching yourself on television giving a pre-recorded interview) is effectively a fragmentation of self, or 'self-multiplication'. Therefore, think what it must be like to be famous, and in tens of thousands of places at once! Gergen's ideas are echoed by Vonk and Ashmore's 'multifaceted self'[22] and by the earlier work of Rom Harré,[23] who introduces the concept of 'file selves', which are aspects of self which reproduce and continue to interact socially away from the body, for example, a job application form.

Harré is also careful to point out that there is a difference between the private experience of self and the public presentation of self, normally referred to as *identity*.[24] This is an important point, since the two terms are frequently confused in psychology, and it could be argued that, while we are aware of many different 'selves' which we present publicly, most of us are also conscious of a core self, sometimes referred to as 'true self'.[25] Perhaps *social* aspects of self are better contained within an overall concept of 'identity'. Indeed, this is the preferred term in much contemporary research.

Popular music and 'the self'

Whether it is universal or not, fragmenting or not, 'peculiar' or not, the idea of a core, 'true self' is very much alive in modern (Western) society and is a major factor in the kind of psychological crises that lie in wait for the famous and celebrated.

Where Gergen's theory of the 'modernist' self is most clearly demonstrated in celebrity culture is in talk directed towards the revelation (or otherwise) of a celebrity's 'true' character. If selves are there to be measured through psychometric instruments, 'teased out' in therapy, and 'discovered' through tree-hugging in the Appalachians, then speculation should be rife about whether or not celebrities are revealing their true self in the spotlight of the media.

Popular music, in particular, has an obsession with the *authenticity* of self. Pop has, from the start, been characterized by artificiality and camp posturing; at the start of the 1960s the industry was dominated by record producers such as Phil Spector and Joe Meek: the 'artists' (that is, the singers and musicians) were merely pretty faces that would look good on television and on record sleeves. During the 1960s, however, the concept of the singer-songwriter (for example, Bob Dylan), and more sophisticated, relatively autonomous acts such as the Beatles and the Rolling Stones, brought about a change in the way pop was talked and written about. Suddenly a divide began to open up between 'serious artists' and 'commercial' performers.

Although pop stars had always come in for the 'Hollywood' treatment, with a focus on the personalities behind the music, now a more serious type of publication began to emerge, such as *Melody Maker* and the *New Musical Express* in the UK and, later, *Rolling Stone* in America. The 'rock weeklies', as they became known, were interested in more than the singer's favourite colour and the details of their first kiss. Interest began to concentrate on the lyrics to the songs, which were becoming more sophisticated and more personal; and, where appropriate, their opinions on all matters from politics to sex to the merits (or otherwise) of their contemporaries. Suddenly the pop star was more than just a pretty face: s/he was a seer figure in the tradition of famous names through history.

There is a very good reason why this might have happened, and it is contained in the nature of the pop lyric itself. No other art form allows the artist to expose his or her 'inner self' quite so brazenly. Poets must codify their musings in allegory and metaphor; novelists and film-makers in the guise of fiction; visual artists by abstract representational forms. The three-minute pop song is a *carte blanche* for the lyricist to bare his or her soul. It doesn't happen all the time, of course; most lyricists prefer to write about sex or dancing. Some deliberately write in the first person from contrary perspectives, such as Paul Weller or Morrissey. Occasionally, however, a lyricist will write, as s/he sees it, straight from the heart. There is also some empirical evidence to suggest that fame itself produces a marked increase in 'self-consciousness'. American psychologist Mark Schaller has studied the work of a number of songwriters and found a significant increase in the number of first-person pronouns in accordance with an increase in the author's fame.[26]

Perhaps the most dramatic example of the latent 'soul-searching' lyric was provided by Kevin Rowland, the singer and songwriter with Dexys Midnight Runners, a British band from the 1980s. Piqued by his early confrontations with the rock weeklies, and recognizing the opportunity for a Barnumesque publicity stunt, Rowland announced the arrival of his band in 1980 not by doing the usual round of press interviews but by issuing a series of 'essays' in the form of advertisements, in which he outlined the musical philosophy of his project. (Dexys never were more than a glorified backing band, or musical vehicle, for Rowland himself – he hired and fired at will and went through at least three completely different line-ups.) Although the hated journalists would have been only too happy to administer a sound critical pasting, the first LP was strong enough to receive unanimously favourable reviews.

When Dexys returned two years later, Rowland's existential angst was channelled into the songs themselves. The 1982 LP *Too-Rye-Ay* contains some of the most remarkably personal lyrics ever committed to audiotape. Throughout, the emphasis is on the disillusionment of adulthood, such as his attempt to recapture childhood happiness in *Until I Believe in my Soul*: 'on the train from New Street to Euston, and back to Harrow again/ Trying to get the feeling that I had back in 1972'. On another track (*I'll Show You*) he wonders whatever happened to the bad boys at school 'who swapped dirty pictures and talked during prayers?' He enlightens us: 'Alcoholics, child molesters, nervous wrecks, prima donnas'. Alas, Rowland himself, despite having been so nice and polite, is left only with his childhood memories. In *Liars A to E* he feels strongly enough to be self-effacing, picturing a pack of journalists lying in wait: 'Here comes his "soul", get your pen and notebooks ready'. On *Until I Believe In My Soul* he even breaks into a sob for added effect. In the history of fame, Rowland was a throwback to the hermits and holy men who reject society to nourish the soul. But by choosing pop as his medium, he ran an awful risk of being ridiculed. The fact that he emerged from the experience critically unscathed speaks volumes for the quality of the music.

I have elaborated here to demonstrate an example of the psychological knife-edge that pop music has become. Heaven forbid that anyone should fail to take Kevin Rowland seriously, and yet the artifice, the camp posturing that is pop's tradition, continues to be the dominant style of expression in pop music for a variety of reasons and, as postmodernist theorists continually remind us, the barriers between the camp and the serious have long since been breached. Therefore it has become highly important for the serious acts to display total authenticity.

The worst crime a 'serious' band or artist can commit is to *sell out*. This accusation is usually levelled at an act that has produced one or two highly acclaimed, original, but commercially unsuccessful records before embarking on a string of hit singles aimed at the mass market. Traditionally, the sell-out is accompanied by a radical change in image, to fit in with a popular contemporary style. The discourse of authenticity is so entrenched in popular music that, typically, bands furiously deny having undergone any changes aimed at selling more records.

During the 1989-90 period in Britain there was a vogue for 'indie-dance music' following the popularity of Acid House and dance music clubs in general during the late 1980s. At the time (as happens periodically in British pop), it was argued that traditional guitar bands were in decline, until Manchester bands the Stone Roses and Happy Mondays had sudden, unexpected hit singles, entering the chart simultaneously in early 1989. Both bands, while sticking to the 1960s format of the pop group, and (more particularly the Stone Roses) having traditional pop influences, also paid explicit homage to dance music. When one or two other bands had hits subsequently with records in a similar style, the term 'indie-dance' was coined by the rock press and before long it became, in rock journalist parlance, a 'bandwagon'. Previously unfashionable rock bands cast off their leathers overnight, pulling on brightly coloured baggy clothing, roping in trendy club DJs to produce their records, claiming that they had always been influenced by dance music. When I dared to suggest, in a review for *Music Week*, that one particular band had been guilty of such a transformation, I, along with my editor and the band's PR agent, was sent an angry letter from the band's management demanding a retraction of the accusation (I am proud to say that, in time-honoured journalistic fashion, the letter was haughtily ignored).

Rock'n'roll suicide

At a superficial level, this quest for authenticity simply adds to the fun of the pop circus and provides another stitch in the tapestry of the perpetual artist–critic struggle. However, at an individual level, it constitutes another crisis for the celebrity, which is all the more acute for the ammunition it gives critics, and thus the lack of the celebrity's power to control it. At its most extreme it can constitute a life-or-death scenario.

There is a long history of artistic suicide as a means to ending the private–public self anguish. The earliest recorded instance is Thomas Chatterton, an eighteenth-century English boy who committed suicide aged 17 after his failure to gain recognition for 'discovering' an unknown fifteenth-century poet. The poems were, as it turned out by his own admission, written by none other than Chatterton himself. For some time afterwards, Chatterton symbolized the importance of art and the expression of the self for writers such as Wordsworth and Coleridge, although, as the critic Hazlitt suggested, his suicide may have been little more than a career move, as his poems weren't much good anyway. But it was a clear sign that the idea of fame for its own sake – the fame of the individual rather than any deeds or achievements – was something worth dying for.

The 'fame of the moment' characterized by the twentieth century has made the need to be discovered in one's lifetime even more important than in Chatterton's day. The ghastly prospect of *losing fame* has been an eternal preoccupation.

There are numerous cases of former professional footballers and, particularly, cricketers, who have found life intolerable after enforced retirement.[27] Terrified by the possibility of losing fame, artists have often resorted to what Keith Simonton[28] calls 'self-handicapping', producing an excuse for not rescaling the heights of their earlier work. After publishing *In Cold Blood* Truman Capote spent the remainder of his life in an alcoholic haze. More dramatically, American writer Thomas Heggen had some success with his debut novel *Mr Roberts*. But he could never match it, and finally decided that suicide was the only viable alternative to artistic obscurity.

As the poet Fulke Greville wrote, as long ago as the seventeenth century, fame is 'hard gotten, worse to keepe / Is never lost but with despaire and shame' (*An Inquisition upon Fame and Honour*). The outcome? 'Some in self-pitty, some in exile languish / Others revell, some kill themselves in anguish.' Perhaps the most tragic celebrity suicide of all was that of Robert O'Donnell, an American paramedic who in 1987 saved an 18-month-old girl trapped in a mine shaft and became a national hero thanks to the massive media interest the case generated, resulting in a TV movie and book. However, stories about 'have-a-go heroes' enjoy a relatively short shelf life even by today's frantic standards. While others eventually return happily to hoeing their garden, O'Donnell was unable to cope with his fading star, and six years later he ended it all.[29]

But the artistic suicide that has most in common with those of popular music stars is that of Ernest Hemingway. Early in his writing career Hemingway had fled from the States to avoid the publicity that his early success had engendered, and poured scorn on others whom he perceived as less modest about their achievements: Scott Fitzgerald he criticized for being 'crazy for immortality', and the 'Bloomsbury crowd' of contemporary writers were, he claimed, more interested in being well-known than for the quality of their work. But the success of his flight from the prying eyes of the media was short-lived: before long the rumours about his private life were circulating, and the more Hemingway tried to preserve the distinction between his life and his work, the harder he found it to cope with life. His suicide was the 'final act of cohesion...in a fragmentation of self and public image'.[30] Braudy contrasts Hemingway with Picasso, a figure from a different (European) tradition, whose identity is a flexible resource, expressed through many different styles and parodies.

The Hemingway/Picasso comparison is loudly echoed by a very modern case of artistic suicide, that of Nirvana singer-songwriter Kurt Cobain. Probably because of the relative size of the two countries, the United States has always lagged somewhat behind Britain when it comes to developments in popular music. Throughout the 1980s it had failed to produce a Morrissey-type seer figure who, for however brief a period, became a spokesperson for disaffected youth. Then, suddenly, along came Nirvana, whose hit single *Smells Like Teen Spirit* thrust the band into the public eye and spearheaded a wave of bands who drew their influences from both punk and heavy metal – a form of music dubbed 'grunge' by the media.

The single became an anthem for a generation, and before long Cobain, as the band's figurehead, was receiving the kind of adulation from fans that quickly became unwelcome – desperate teenagers needing advice, people on the verge of breakdown who feel they cannot confide in anyone but their idol. Cobain soon began to find the pressures of fame hard to handle. 'It was frightening. It scared me', he told a reporter, on finding out just how famous he was. The band's next LP, *In Utero*, was deliberately uncommercial, in an attempt to throw opportunist fans off the scent, and re-establish some of that precious 'authenticity' for the band's long-standing and loyal following. Needless to say, this only intensified Nirvana's cult status. Like many modern celebrities, Cobain's solution to the problem was to escape through drugs, having to curtail a European tour after overdosing on a cocktail of drugs and alcohol. Later, he was referred to a rehabilitation centre for heroin addiction (but then ran away). In April 1994 he was discovered dead on the floor of his Seattle home, having fired a bullet through his brain.

Cobain's case shares similarities with most of the suicides and premature deaths that have littered the (relatively) short history of commercial popular music. Hard drugs invariably play a large part in the outcome, and yet drug-taking is rife throughout the music business, and cannot explain all the untimely deaths, especially where the victim is a regular and knowledgeable user of the substance. It is perhaps in the explanatory note Cobain left behind at the scene of his death that we find some of the clues to his demise. Penned to an imaginary childhood friend, 'Boddah', he moves quickly on to the problems of establishing 'independence' and 'the embracement of your community'. He should have learned the lessons, he says, of the history of 'punk rock'. The crux of the message is that he feels he is letting his fans down through his inability to derive any enjoyment from making music.

> For example, when we're backstage and the lights go out and the manic roar of the crowd begins, it doesn't affect me the way in which it did for Freddy Mercury, who seemed to love, relish in the love and adoration from the crowd, which is something I totally admire and envy. The fact is, I can't fool you, any one of you. It simply isn't fair to you or me. The worst crime I can think of would be to rip people off by faking it and pretending as if I'm having 100% fun.[31]

Cobain's reference to Freddie Mercury is very interesting, for Mercury is Picasso to Cobain's Hemingway. Mercury, the lead singer with British band Queen, died from AIDS-related illness in 1992. He was the ultimate camp showman, the arch parodist of musical styles from 1920s music hall to heavy metal, funk and rock'n'roll. His lyrics were (mostly) pure pastiche. For him, music was as much about performance as about posterity, while Cobain was trapped in the desperate desire for authenticity, for giving his 'real self' to his most committed followers. Insincerity is the ultimate crime, and he decided that, like Hemingway, he would rather be dead than insincere.

Film critic Richard Dyer suggests that the quest for authenticity so dear to serious pop stars may have its roots in the world of the cinema. He describes it as 'a quality necessary to the star phenomenon to make it work'.[32] The importance of sincerity has made it more important than other factors, such as acting (or musical) skill, or moral or political worth. Lying, as Cobain argued, is the most heinous crime a star can commit. Why is sincerity so important? Dyer suggests it is the reassurance for the public that a performer's success is due to some elusive quality – 'charisma', 'star quality', or a 'gift', and 'grounded in her own immediate (= not controlled), spontaneous (= unpremeditated) and essential (= private) self'.[33]

Another suicide similar to Cobain's is that of Richey Edwards, guitarist in the Welsh band Manic Street Preachers. (I use the term 'suicide' advisedly here; no body has been found, yet all the signs point to that conclusion.) Edwards was another pop star with a high level of drug use, although this was compounded by severe anorexia and clinically diagnosed depression which forced him to be hospitalized at least once during his career. His disappearance was the culmination of a downward spiral of increasingly erratic behaviour.[34] Eventually he was reported missing from a London hotel early in 1995, and his car was found abandoned near the Severn Bridge on the English–Welsh border, a popular suicide location.

That any number of psychological factors could explain Edwards' case is not in doubt. Nonetheless, he was a man with a keen sense of the need for authenticity. Early in the band's career they encountered BBC radio presenter Steve Lamacq (then a music journalist) at a concert, who was casting doubts about their seriousness as a rock group, and accusing them of parody. No problem if you are a Picasso or a Freddie Mercury; but it was too much for Edwards who, backstage, suddenly produced a penknife and gradually carved the expression '4 REAL' into his forearm, thus leaving the open-jawed reporter in little doubt as to the band's sincerity.

Commodification

One of the most alienating aspects of the star system is the potential loss of *control*, a major source of distress for celebrities. While this is a particular problem if 'authenticity' is a key motif in a star's career, all celebrities are faced with the harsh reality that their success is making someone else rich, and in the eyes of their employers they can be little more than unit-shifting sources of capital. This process has been referred to as the 'commodification' of the self.[35]

> As soon as I went to number one, everything went mad. I went from a person to a product – bam! Just like that. I became a 'star' even to my best friends and family. They didn't seem to be able to communicate with me on any other level except as some weird sort of, I dunno, famous object. [Sinead O'Connor][36]

The impression of being a product rather than a person also extends to the cotton-wool environment of record companies and football clubs. Like the Hollywood studio that dictated Myrna Loy's character right down to even the most trivial public exchange (going to the shops), the institutions that preserve and cocoon celebrities can become stifling:

> I can't even open a door for myself. I walk in a room and just put my arms out, and the coat's on, and I don't even have to button it. Everybody does everything for me all the time. [rock star Alice Cooper][37]

One phenomenon that could be attributed to cocooning is the 'bad' and bizarre behaviour alluded to in Chapter 1. When you inhabit an environment where you don't even have to button your own coat, it is not altogether surprising that you become surly and spoilt and make unreasonable demands on everyone around you. This sense of being 'taken away' from normality is a major step in the commodification process. One of the important developments in this period is in the evolution of myths surrounding the celebrity which start to gnaw away at the individual's presentation of self. This is precisely the same dilemma that beset Hemingway (whose ability to control the mythologizing was, ironically, impaired by his decision to run away from it). The myths can therefore establish the celebrity as a particular type of person in the public eye, a presentation of self over which we have little control, as the actor Marlon Brando found to his cost:

> Fame has been the bane of my life, and I would gladly have given it up. I have been forced to live a false life, and all the people I know, with the exception of a handful, have been affected by my being famous. People don't relate to you but to the myth they think you are, and the myth is always wrong.[38]

Eventually this commodification does have a crucial impact on the celebrity's sense of self; as the above quotes demonstrate, celebrities feel that the myth infects all their social interaction – not just their dealings with the media but friends and family as well. There are many instances of famous people referring to themselves in the third person (even Julius Caesar had a habit of referring to himself as 'Caesar'!). An even more spectacular way of dealing with the sense of commodification is actively to create alternative 'selves' for different contexts:

> In my eyes this book's not about me...it's about all the photographers and the people that never get the credit, like make-up artists,

and hairdressers and stylists... If I look good in a picture, it doesn't mean to say it's a good picture. There are incredible pictures and I just see them as that. I don't see me in the pictures as me. ['supermodel' Kate Moss][39]

There is Chris Eubank the fighter and there is Chris Eubank who is talking to you now who is a far different personality. He is a personality which is true, which is real and above all he is good.[40]

In the above quote, Kate Moss is quite clearly disowning her commodified self by accepting the photographs as objects which are both media products and works of art. Chris Eubank is more explicit about his dual public image: a boxer who has stirred up controversy by denigrating his sport, he sees his fighting role as pure performance, but at the same time clings to the notion of 'authenticity' in his public presentation of self beyond the ring. Whether there is a third Chris Eubank (whose habitat is the domestic sphere) is another question.

Some support for this idea comes from a study by Adler and Adler,[41] who examined the impact of becoming famous on the self-concept of US college basketball players over a five-year period. It was argued that the pressures of media involvement, and the increased number of relationships their incipient fame imposed upon them, forced them to expand their sense of self, culminating in the creation of a 'gloried self' which began to function as a kind of alter ego. One participant, in relating a regrettable incident, remarked: 'That ain't like me. That was Apollo [his gloried self] that done that, not me.'[42] However the authors argue that, rather than maintaining these other selves, the athletes eventually integrated them into their 'core selves'. Nevertheless, these other selves may be exclusively reserved for performance, as suggested by the use of pseudonyms, or 'stage names'.

In the history of celebrity, the use of the pseudonym may indicate a distancing of public self from private self. Many journalists use pseudonyms for tax-evasion purposes, but some use them as a means of creating a print persona which is radically different from their social identity. Similarly, stars may treat their performing selves as a dramatic role, so that taking the stage – even in an 'authentic' capacity as a singer or comedian – becomes a dramatic performance. The following quote, from entertainer Freddie Starr, suggests that the persona represented by the pseudonym may be closer to the 'real self' than initially intended:

> We're all human beings. I don't believe in the word 'star'. Never have done. Just put bums on seats and I'm only Freddie Starr when the band strikes up and the curtain goes up and it's like breaking out of prison.[43]

Trying to maintain a consistent sense of 'true self' is made particularly difficult in the initial stages of fame, when the celebrity finds herself caught up in a dizzying whirl of social interaction. In Chapter 3 I described a possible scenario in which a pop singer replicates herself thousands of times through various media outlets; as she enters all these (parasocial) relationships, the sense of true self becomes harder and harder to cling on to. As the singer Sade comments:

> Everything starts again, in a way. You've been used to living in a certain way and being a certain person, sort of quite extrovert if anything, always fooling around, always trying to make people laugh. And when you're conscious that people know exactly who you are, you have a feeling, you know, that you want to be quite low-key, because you don't want to give them more than they already think they have. So you tend to get a bit more mousey, or I did.[44]

This is particularly true in the context of the media interview, in which a celebrity is asked questions relating to their private life (as the opening of the book suggests, 'private' life is perhaps not the best term to describe the everyday experience of a celebrity). Here, Gergen argues, people are transformed into 'spectacles' which threaten 'the very concept of the substantial or true self...when my "personal" opinion is polished for public consumption it ceases to be personal.'[45]

Other writers have argued that, for public figures, identity is clearly a performance. In one study it was shown how celebrity disc jockey Tony Blackburn was able to summon up a whole range of different 'voices' within the context of a brief phone interview, each bearing the stamp of a distinct identity.[46] His 'DJ voice', for example, was characterized by a rising pitch at the end of a sentence where one might expect falling intonation (a similar device can be seen in the interviews given by highly media-trained modern sports stars). Other voices included an 'empathetic voice' designed to display sympathy in serious moments of disclosure from interviewees, and a 'camp/send-up voice' to signal that he is adopting a contrary position to the one we might expect 'the real Tony Blackburn' to hold. It has been said that giving an interview is as much a part of public performance as singing on stage or boxing in the ring.[47] Therefore, in these two chapters I have been careful to select quotes from fairly reliable media sources, where interviews have been conducted one-to-one and at some length, and published as a serious feature article in a broadsheet newspaper or magazine. My argument for accepting these quotes at face value is that in-depth interviews with 'respected' (that is, non-tabloid) journalists are treated as *confessionals* by celebrities, and thus serve a radically different function from the televised interview, or a schedule reported in a news letter. Of course there *are* situations (particularly where substantial amounts of money are involved) where a celebrity grants an interview to a media outlet and announces that this is an opportunity to deliver the 'truth', and here we must be more sceptical.

Conclusion

In this chapter I have begun to turn attention to the strange world inhabited by the modern celebrity. Given that fame is largely the celebration of the individual, it has been necessary to examine how a private sense of self might be affected by fame, not to mention one's sense of identity in the many public performances of celebrity life. A key theme throughout the history of fame, but one that has gained increasing importance in the twentieth century, has been the notion of 'authenticity'. When this is threatened, by the commercial demands of modern showbusiness, the results can be tragic, as characterized by the suicide of Kurt Cobain and other stars. At a less dramatic level, many find that the only way to deal with the commodification process of celebrity is to create alternative 'selves' to conduct the presentation of identity in selected contexts.

However, existential concerns are not the only ways in which fame can be a burden, and the next chapter considers some more of the 'problems' of being a celebrity.

Chapter 6
The problems of being famous

The fourteenth-century Florentine poet Petrarch would have sympathized with the plight of the modern celebrity as he travelled through Europe beset by ardent fans, forcing their poems upon him. Greta Garbo was among the first of the modern celebrities to revolt openly against the pressures of dealing with the general public, so much so that she spent many periods of her career 'in hiding', and even took to donning disguises to avoid recognition.[1] Needless to say, such attempts frequently ended in failure, with stories of her being chased around Central Park by the press and having to be smuggled into her hotel, and of reporters hiring hotel personnel as private detectives (a common occurrence today). 'The story of my life is about back entrances and side doors and secret elevators and other ways of getting in and out of places so that people won't bother you.'[2]

The focus in this chapter is on the way celebrities 'problematize' fame. Apart from the existential anguish that compromising 'authenticity' may bring, there are a number of social issues that celebrities must deal with if they are to cope with the pressures of being famous. Meeting people is one of the biggest hazards they face, especially with people who appear regularly on television. I sometimes find, in my role as a university lecturer, that people come up to me on campus and talk to me as though they know me, even though I am sure that I do not know *them*. But, as a lecturer, you have a simple explanation available: that person is one of your students, whose relationship with you is parasocial inasmuch as it has been conducted simultaneously with 100 other parasocial relationships in a lecture theatre. For a television personality or soap star, this feeling of being known, but not *knowing* people, may extend to every third person you pass in the street.

In Charlie Chaplin's autobiography,[3] he describes at some length the negative emotions induced by the attentions of hordes of fans, and not even fans: 'At the height of my popularity', he wrote, 'friends and acquaintances crowded in on me excessively.'[4] Chaplin first encountered public adoration early in his career, when he travelled across the United States by train for work purposes and found himself the reluctant centre of attention. This passage offers some telling insights into the experience of pre-war celebrity, at a time when the public's awareness of the mass media was not sufficiently advanced for stars to be continuously recognized in the street, but if news got around that there was a star in the vicinity, scenes bordering on mass hysteria might develop.

Certainly, at the time of Chaplin's train journey, communications were sufficiently swift for news of his imminent arrival to reach locations more quickly than the train, thus enabling local residents to turn out in force to greet him. He was repeatedly mobbed by fans on his arrival at various locations, and people even waved from fields as the train passed by.

> I wanted to enjoy it all without reservation, but I kept thinking the world had gone crazy! If a few slapstick comedies could arouse such excitement, was there not something bogus about all celebrity? I had always thought I would like the public's attention, and here it was – paradoxically isolating me with a depressing sense of loneliness.[5]

The complaint of 'loneliness' by celebrities is a common one, and will recur a number of times later in this chapter.

New relationships

> I have very, very few friends. I live in a very tight circle and emotionally I'm probably not as generous as I once was. In an average week I probably meet 150 new people and that's uncomfortable sometimes. They know who I am, but I can't remember their names, and that makes me worry that I'm not treating this person well. [Veronica Webb, a 'supermodel'][6]

Probably the single most important cause of unhappiness reported by celebrities is the effect of having to deal with so many people all the time. The loss of privacy is one aspect of this, and will be explored in more detail in the following section. But fame forces us to enter into so many new relationships that the sheer number of these can itself be a stressful experience. As suggested earlier, the more social interactions we have, the more we have to compromise our 'true' selves – eventually something snaps, and the rudeness and arrogance which is often attributed to celebrities is undoubtedly the outcome of having to deal with so many people that the mask of courtesy occasionally slips.

There is little doubt that you and I engage in more relationships than our ancestors did. It is estimated that in the Middle Ages the average person only ever *saw* 100 different individuals in the course of a lifetime.[7] Today, television can bring 100 new faces into one's life in a matter of seconds. Even if we discount parasocial interaction, technological advances and the corresponding changes in society have meant that time and space are no obstacles to forming relationships. As we move through life, the cast of relevant characters is ever-expanding. For some this means an ever-increasing sense of stress. 'How can we be friends with them? We don't have time for the friends we already have!'[8]

In previous centuries, relationships were determined by proximity and little else. When someone left the village to live elsewhere, that person disappeared from your life – unless they were kin or a close friend, in which case you might have used letters to maintain an 'epistolary' relationship. Again, we need to search for evolutionary explanations for managing people. Humankind has evolved by dealing with small numbers of acquaintances in work and play, most of those blood related, and then along comes the telephone, the video camera, rapid and cheap transportation, the Internet, and suddenly it seems we can be friends with anyone and everyone. How quickly can we really expect to adapt our behaviour to these circumstances?

There is a large body of research on relationships *per se*, much of it focusing solely on relationships within the nuclear family (such as parent–child interaction), and an equally large body of psychodynamic research into relationships, though much of this is concerned only with relationship pathology. Some work has however been carried out studying relationship networks, particularly by Robert Milardo, who has identified a number of types of network for each individual.[9] Each individual can identify a number of 'significant others' who are considered highly important in everyday interaction; an 'exchange network' of people who provide support; an 'interaction network' of people we have interactions with; and a 'global network' comprising everyone who is known to us. In a diary study, student participants reported having a surprisingly low average of 4.6 'social episodes' each day, and appeared to have an interactive network of, on average, around 26 people.[10] Global networks have, so far, proved harder to research.[11] Indeed, it may be impossible, and futile, to speculate about 'norms' with regard to social networks, since so many other factors – socio-cultural background, individual preferences – are likely to influence their size and shape.

Nevertheless, the question of how we manage relationships in times of rapid technological change is an important one, and certainly, for the average celebrity, the situation is critical. In the early stages of fame, the number of people a celebrity has to deal with rapidly swells to enormous proportions, featuring not only other celebrities and their supporting cast of managers, agents and PR employees, but also millions of television viewers and newspaper readers. Therefore, there may be a need to identify a fifth social network, maybe even a 'virtual network', which includes all the people who *know* an individual (regardless of whether the individual knows them).[12]

However, you may argue, isn't this expansion of relationships one of the strongest motivational factors for fame? Might we not become famous in order to meet the rich, successful and beautiful? For some celebrities, this is undoubtedly a major spur. When the entertainer Rolf Harris met the Queen, for example, it seems he could barely contain his excitement:

> And like, with the Queen, when she pinned on my OBE, she discussed my career with me with such knowledge about what I was doing, it was unbelievable! She knew the whole history of my career. It was bloody amazing![13]

Having the Queen strike up a parasocial relationship with you is an achievement in itself. If even the Queen cannot ignore you, then there must be a substantial number of rich, successful and beautiful people who feel they know you intimately. Unfortunately, for every rich, successful or beautiful person, there are thousands of people with whom you might have little interest in cultivating relationships. This is potentially a major problem for anyone who becomes famous, especially if they are not always at ease in convivial social situations where there is much 'small talk' and superficial interaction. The situation is summed up succinctly by Adam Duritz, singer with the briefly famous Counting Crows:

> If you have trouble dealing with people and you get famous, then you've just got more people to have trouble with. The thing is, when you become a 'star', you suddenly get to meet all these people you might have admired for a long time. But if you're in a room with 100 people, there might be five you'd enjoy meeting and would get along with, and they're probably not the ones you're going to meet. The way it works is that, at this stage of my life, all 100 of them have no qualms about coming up and talking to me, and most of them don't really understand what I'm doing, either.[14]

The first stages of fame are characterized by an increasing number of social gatherings such as the one alluded to in the above quote. Given that fame (in contemporary society) emerges through media coverage, many of these gatherings will be media-related, such as press conferences, and 'photo shoots'. New celebrities can endure these occasions without too much discomfort because they are temporary, and there are usually a number of people (such as press officers) who are able to shepherd them through.

It is during the next stages of fame that the problems begin: when complete strangers, who have formed parasocial relationships with celebrities, begin to encounter them in public places. A common complaint by celebrities is that they feel as though their 'personal space' is being invaded. Stuart Cosgrove, a journalist who experienced a modicum of fame as a radio personality, described this experience:

> You go out with close friends and you end up spending the whole evening talking to strangers about jokes you cracked on the radio. I took a train from Edinburgh to Glasgow one Friday night and eight people talked to me about the show. Even the man selling tea and

sandwiches sat down and chatted for about 20 minutes. You don't get any space... I spend more time hiding now.[15]

After a while, the invasion of space becomes too great for celebrities to feel entirely comfortable in public places: as tennis star Monica Seles commented (before she was attacked): 'You can't go out. You just go to the hotel.'[16] TV chef Keith Floyd puts it even more graphically:

> You get frightened to go out. People you'd like to speak to don't speak to you because they're too polite to interfere with your privacy. People you don't want to speak to hound you to death. Everybody thinks you're incredibly rich when you're not. And... there is no-one to talk to. That is the trouble with being a celebrity. No-one believes you if you say you're lonely or you're worried or you're depressed.[17]

This complaint of loneliness echoes that reported by Charlie Chaplin earlier in the chapter. Loneliness has been described as the *feeling* of isolation, as opposed to isolation itself, and this can often be caused by the absence of a confidant, or of a 'reliable alliance' – someone who can be trusted in times of anxiety.[18] The complaint of loneliness as the result of fame is not restricted to modern celebrity: Cicero, in 60 BC, complained that, despite the 'droves of friends' surrounding him, he was unable to find one with whom he could 'fetch a private sigh'.[19] Centuries later, Rousseau echoes the sentiment: 'As soon as I had a name, I ceased to have friends.'[20] The process of fame plants an element of distrust in the celebrity's relationships. On meeting each new acquaintance, the question becomes not so much, 'Does this person like me for who I am?' but 'Does this person like me for *what* I am?'

Looked at another way, the problem of celebrity loneliness may be linked to Sinead O'Connor's earlier remark that even family and friends began to relate to her as a star when her record reached number one. The loneliness may well result from the dispersion of self; if you have produced thousands of copies of yourself, which replications do people find themselves interacting with? The likelihood is that even your closest companions will interact with your replicated selves some of the time, and that this will interfere with their relationship to you as a single, unified person.

The loss of privacy

While fame can create the feeling of psychological distance from friends and family, it can create the reverse effect of feeling that there is nowhere to hide. Perhaps the most common of all celebrity complaints is the loss of privacy. This is almost certainly connected to the recognition of the celebrity by the general public. Little research has been carried out into the management of relationship networks by individuals, and yet it would seem likely that most of us find we have a distinct threshold of intimacy. For example, the lifelong resident of a small village will greet passers-by in the street even if they are strangers, because she will recognize most of the people she sees and it seems natural to extend this familiarity to all human beings. By contrast, a city dweller would soon find it exhausting and unrewarding to keep up this kind of behaviour.

At some point, the threshold is crossed when we become famous and are recognized constantly by strangers. Here it becomes apparent that we are no longer able to manage our personal space as we would like. This is compounded by the fact that these strangers know more about ourselves than we would like them to, creating a potentially more unwelcome situation than one in which attention is simply drawn to one as a result of some unusual feature (such as an outrageous hat or hairstyle). In the published diaries of the actor Kenneth Williams, he describes a typical encounter with the public:

> We went to the Odeon at Edgware Road to see a film but a crowd of hooligans shouted 'Hallo Kenny, you queer!' and more in this vein till I got up and went over to them and asked 'Who is making these remarks? And who has the guts to stand up and say them to my face?' and there was silence. God! Why don't people leave one alone?[21]

Most of Williams's unpleasant experiences involving members of the public seemed to stem from strangers' knowledge about, and hostility towards, his homosexuality. However public abuse needs no extra fuel than preconceptions about the celebrity lifestyle, as a quote from the singer Robbie Williams suggests:

> I come off the train, I get abuse, three or four times a week. I have a theory about the media, and people's dull minds. Apparently, I'm

having such a fucking great time and I'm earning such great money, that everything's a bowl of cherries, so there's a lot of hatred.[22]

The loss of privacy is most often cited in conjunction with the intrusive behaviour of the press. In the scenario outlined in Chapter 1, I described a situation which celebrities often report, where the curtains of the building they are in are permanently closed for fear that a photographer with a long lens will take a picture of them. This seems ironic, given the hunger for publicity that drives so many to seek fame. But perhaps the single most problematic aspect of fame is the continuous attention that never abates, even in one's most intimate moments.

The intrusion of the press is nowhere better exemplified than in the case of Diana, Princess of Wales. Much of the reportage following her death in August 1997 featured phrases like 'literally hounded to death'. Although a multitude of fanciful conspiracy theories have sprouted in the meantime, it is certain that the immediate cause of her death was directly related to the pursuit of the mobile paparazzi. Why should someone like Diana, acclimatized to constant media attention as she was, still feel threatened by the press?

Evidently this need for privacy – at least a private space that one can enter at will – is a fundamental human requirement. Or is it? Again, we need to turn to cross-cultural psychology for evidence of societies which differ from the Western world, and the anthropologist Clifford Geertz describes the situation in Java:

> There are no walls or fences around [the houses], the house walls are thinly and loosely woven, and there are commonly not even doors. Within the house people wander freely just about any place any time, and even outsiders wander in fairly freely almost any time during the day and early evening. In brief, privacy in our terms is about as close to nonexistent as it can get. You may walk freely into a room where a man or woman is stretched out (clothed, of course) sleeping. You may enter from the rear of the house as well as from the front, with hardly more warning than a greeting announcing your presence.[23]

This (to Westerners) wholly unfamiliar situation suggests that the environment in which one is raised shapes our meanings of privacy. In many societies, both contemporary and historical, privacy seems to be correlated with wealth and prestige; in other words, private space is a privilege rather than a basic human right. This is reflected in the development of select housing estates for the rich in the United States, surrounded by fortress-like boundaries and protected by armed guards. The social history of Western culture can be traced through the emergence of boundaries and the increased distinction between private (inside, nuclear, family-based) and public (outside).[24]

The importance attached to privacy in Western society is, therefore, related to our domestic arrangements, particularly the way in which the internal organization of family homes has changed over the centuries.[25] Indeed, it has been argued that the modern concept of 'private life' did not emerge until the eighteenth century.[26] Consider the way in which children are raised in many homes in modern Britain and North America, where it is quite common for a child to inhabit a single bedroom until they leave the parental home. The single bedroom is a space of great significance in the development of self and identity. It is a shrine to privacy; it is an asylum where one can shelter from conflicts with parents or other siblings; it is a safe haven where one can cultivate hobbies and interests, decorate the walls with pictures and other symbols which serve to create a social identity, listen to one's private collection of music, and assemble one's personal wardrobe; and, increasingly, use the telephone to conduct private conversations with other teenagers or watch the programmes of one's choice on a personal television set.[27]

So great a part of one's teenage years is spent in this private space it is no wonder that leaving home is so traumatic for older teenagers, especially if it involves sharing accommodation. Indeed, a young celebrity may never go through the experience of leaving the parental home (and, therefore, their sacred private space), and so the intrusion of the cameras and the general public may be a violation of personal space that is extremely hard to negotiate.

The cause of most distress related to privacy invasion seems to be the off-guard photograph, snatched in a seemingly private moment. Paparazzi using long lenses frequently catch pictures of (usually female) celebrities baring all on exotic beaches, and these often find their way into prominent positions in one of the next morning's tabloid newspapers. Such pictures are normally purchased and condemned with equal vigour. As much as anything, they provide a glimpse of that 'sacred space', or parallel universe, inhabited by celebrities, and the off-guard photo symbolizes the human-ness of the stars. This type of press photography in fact dates back to pre-war Europe, where a photographer named Erich Salomon gatecrashed major political meetings carrying one of the new lightweight makes of camera, and snapped pictures of world leaders, not in the midst of rhetorical flight but having a crafty fag backstage. As a photographer from that period put it: 'All of these people who had appeared to the public as stuffed shirts, suddenly, there they are, smoking cigars, relaxing, their legs all over the place.'[28]

Another problem for celebrities is that their families – and particularly their partners – are ripe material for press attention. Sometimes this can be welcome (I would hazard a guess that James Major is none too upset by his father's fame!). At other times it can place a relationship under considerable strain. The problems are doubled when two celebrities become romantically involved. When British actor Hugh Grant was arrested in America just as a prostitute was on the point of administering oral sex to him, the media quickly rounded on his celebrity partner Liz Hurley; likewise, when footballer David Beckham returned from the 1998 World Cup to a hostile reception (for getting needlessly sent off against Argentina, adjudged by many to be a turning point for England's chances), he quickly joined partner Victoria 'Posh Spice' Adams on tour in the States, attracting a flurry of unwelcome press attention in her direction.

Of course, the loss of privacy is not necessarily a matter for the individual person; the intrusions of the press also invade the personal space of other people close to a celebrity – partners, children, and other friends and relatives who may receive unwelcome attention. With celebrity couples, the problems are compounded further. In this section I have concentrated on the privacy of individuals, but this can be extended to include a household. In this case the issue is less about being alone than about controlling the boundaries of one's territory, repelling invaders, and a host of other behaviours that may have long-standing evolutionary roots.

Explanations for fame

Once the early stages of fame have been survived, the initial intrusions of privacy have become commonplace, and the recognition of the general public has passed from novel to irritating, to ever-so-slightly wearisome, there may be time for celebrities to reflect on their bizarre experiences. In the extract from Charlie Chaplin's autobiography quoted earlier in this chapter, he found himself reacting to his fame with considerable bemusement. In its adoration for him and his slapstick comedies, it was as though 'the world had gone crazy'.

Today, the idea of slapstick comedy being an odd claim to fame seems absurd in itself. So many people have become famous for so little, individual celebrities have to struggle to account for their own unique fame. Comparisons with fellow stars are often unflattering in the extreme, and being the 'flavour of the month' is not an explanation that is likely to appeal to many celebrities. An alternative approach is to analyse your fame in terms of its social (or media) functions. The entertainer Rolf Harris, for example, can offer little more than the authenticity of his self-presentation:'Well, it's bloody simple really. It's because I've been honest with people through all my career. I've never conned anybody.'[29]

A gas fitter or social worker may read those words and point out that they too have been honest all their life, and nobody knows them from Adam. Of course, Rolf's explanation for his fame is no explanation at all. Cilla Black, another entertainer, attributes her success to nothing more than her *ordinariness*:

> I think they like me because they think they can do it themselves. I can walk into a room and I don't look like Jean Shrimpton [1960s fashion model] and nobody falls down on their knees. And so maybe I give the impression that they can do it. And that's why I'm still here.[30]

Black perceives herself primarily as a role model for the general public rather than an outstanding human being. It is a perfectly acceptable rationale because it would be hard for her to justify earning fame as a reward for exceptional talent; although her earlier fame arose through her singing, her later, and more substantial fame, was earned as a television presenter.

This explanation for the success of television entertainers fits comfortably with Marshall's theory of celebrity as a symbol of democratic capitalism. His 'reading' of Oprah Winfrey relates the appeal of 'ordinariness' to the phenomenon of authenticity discussed in Chapter 5 in relation to pop stars. Oprah's authenticity is not so much an issue for the star as a private individual as for the television producers who are trying to popularize her show. As far as the studio audience is concerned, she 'represents their channel and avenue to public discourse'.[31] Their identification with her as an 'ally' is crucial to the show's success.

Eddie 'The Eagle' Edwards is a man who is famous largely for lacking talent and putting a brave face on it (his exceptional case is described more fully in Chapter 1). It is hard to imagine how someone who owes his success so completely to media hype accounts for his fame. In the following quote, though, he too adopts Cilla Black's (and David Marshall's) argument – that he is popular as a symbol of democratic celebrity:

> There's a number of reasons why I became so popular...One is because the Olympics is all about the taking part – it's not about the winning. But the Olympics has become so professional now, all they're thinking about is money, money, money...and then I come along who is a complete amateur, this great guy who hasn't got any money, no training facilities, no trainer, nothing, but he's still made it to the Olympics, see, and he's just there for the love of his sport and for love of his country and they all love it. And they fall in love with me. I am a symbol of the Olympic spirit. I am a breath of fresh air...And also they could see it was my dream to get to the Olympics and there's a lot of people out there who have sort of dreams like that but they lack the courage and the guts to go out there and grab that dream. But I've made that dream come true and so a lot of people are living their dreams through me. I give them all hope.[32]

Edwards is in no doubt about his role as a 'symbol', or as a conduit for the public's 'dreams'. There is a slight paradox though between both Edwards's and Black's claims that they give the public hope, that 'they can do it', and their images of the public acting out their fantasies vicariously through celebrity exploits. Are Jo and Joe Public wannabe celebrities, or are they content with their parasocial relationships with the stars? Or are they a mixture of the two? The theory seems inconsistent.

Delusions of grandeur: 'We're like God'

In the previous section the celebrities, accounts for their fame seem modest, humble even. In this section I take a look at some slightly more advanced explanations.

In a fascinating paper, Nancy Much and Manamohan Mahapatra describe the 'possession states' entered into by the Kalasis of Orissa in eastern India.[33] Kalasis are individuals who are described as 'conduits for divinity' – at certain periods in their lives they experience possession trances during which they perform a number of rituals which draw the members of the local community into participation with the Gods. During these states, Kalasis lose all attributes of normal consciousness, including their sense of self and memory (the two are, of course, inseparable), and appear entirely to change their outward personality. As the psychologist Nancy Much describes one Kalasi:

> She no longer has the held-in, rounded posture with down-curving shoulders typical of traditional village women. The 'veil' of her sari is now off her head and her walk has become upright and strong-shouldered, a confident, arrogant, even swaggering posture.[34]

What is relevant about Kalasis in the context of celebrity is the way in which the members of the community (the 'supplicants') relate to the Kalasi when they realize (through the enactment of rituals) that she is in her possession state. Through this role as divine conduit, the Kalasi enjoys a social prestige that would otherwise be hard to come by ('these special talents are alternatives to wealth [and] political power... for achieving prestige and enhanced position in society').[35] During the possession state, she has:

> practically absolute social ascendancy over the audience of supplicants. She may command, criticize, scold, demand self-punishments and even whack them lightly with thin canes, as well as predict, advise, comfort, praise, bless, reassure and bestow her loving ministrations on their illnesses and personal problems. Few persons in India, or North America enjoy, even temporarily, such supreme discursive ascendance.[36]

I would suggest that something very similar happens when a person becomes famous in the context of the media. Of course, divinity holds very little sway in modern Western society, so we do not respond to our celebrities as though they were conduits for Gods as such; nevertheless, the process of celebrity bestows a certain amount of prestige on otherwise ordinary individuals that allows them to hold what Much and Mahapatra describe as 'discursive ascendancy' over their supplicants (the consumers of media). The following comments from celebrities need to be interpreted in this light.

> We've got messages... that sounds, like, really corny but deep down I am a hippy. I love the idea of love and happiness for everyone. I love that. And we can spread that to our fans. It may sound corny but we're like God. [Luke Goss of the band Bros][37]

> There is a message in life to be learned from Chris Eubank... He's got so much to offer youngsters. He speaks to youngsters and gets them away from the detrimental things in life, the drugs, the crime. Chris Eubank is a good man and what he says is get away from badness. [Boxer Chris Eubank][38]

> We get thousands of letters a week from people who want some kind of help. I've had people sending me notes saying they're going to commit suicide and I've called them up, and some of them, man, they're beyond help. But you're in this position where you start to think there must be something you can do, you know... It's the same with organisations. We're constantly getting letters asking us to do this or do that. And they're good causes. But they can't even show them to me any more. Because they know I'll let my innards be scooped out. I'll have nothing left. [Eddie Vedder, singer with rock band Pearl Jam][39]

The Luke Goss statement seems laughably pretentious, and yet it is not as preposterous as it may seem for a young man at the peak of his popularity (earned through the performance of a few lightweight pop songs) to search beyond mundane explanations for his unusual new-found status. Ironically, Bros's biggest hit was entitled *When Will I Be Famous?* Chris Eubank sets himself up as a Messiah figure in the second quote, clearly fulfilling the role of the Kalasi; his remarks are particularly interesting given his comment, reported earlier in the chapter, about the two Chris Eubanks – the fighter and the 'good man'. Evidently it is the good man who is spreading the 'message', but ironically it is the fighter who has earned him success and fame.

The third quote, from the lead singer of a successful American rock band, exposes another side of the uneasy relationship between celebrities and the general public – in particular the sense that, as an icon, a celebrity has a *duty*, or a responsibility, to his or her public. I described earlier how one of the aspects of cult status that Kurt Cobain found most difficult to cope with was the deep intimacy of his fanmail, a classic case of a parasocial relationship that has a bilateral dimension (the celebrity cannot help but be drawn into a one-to-one relationship unless s/he has a very harsh screening procedure for dealing with post). This is certainly a problem for the late Cobain's contemporary Eddie Vedder, who is also, he claims, approached by 'organisations' (presumably charitable causes) who want to draw on his support as well.

How much responsibility do celebrities have? How much *should* they have? These questions are difficult to answer, except to point to the intimate relationship between responsibility and power. It's a high cost that comes with supreme discursive ascendancy.

The 'gift': all we want to do is make records...

As discussed earlier, the argument that celebrities became famous as an accidental by-product of their 'gift' is one which has long permeated media discourse. 'Fame, based on an indefinable internal quality of the self, was natural, almost predestined.'[40] Stars are there to be 'discovered', so the argument runs; they have always been special, ever since birth.

There is a fine distinction to be drawn between this belief in an innate gift which will eventually be realized in fame and success, and the claims reported earlier by the likes of Morrissey and Damon Albarn that they 'knew' that they would eventually become famous, or that fame was a kind of *calling* that they felt driven to fulfil. The difference is that the latter type of celebrity has (or *should* have!) few illusions about the outcome – if you always wanted to be famous but you didn't know what for, then any claims to an innate 'gift' can only be made on a *post hoc* basis. It could, conceivably, be argued that the desire for fame was an unconscious acknowledgement of a dormant talent, but this is to take an absurdly deterministic line.

A well-worn argument that celebrities invoke when the pressures of their lives become too much is that they were never in it for the fame to begin with. Eddie Vedder of Pearl Jam again:

> Success on any level can be hard to deal with for most musicians... Because you never really believe you're going to be successful... so when you unexpectedly become more successful than you ever imagined, it can be something that's real heavy to deal with. Because that's not why we got into this. We got into this because we wanted to be in a band, play music, make records.[41]

A similar sentiment is echoed by the actress Sigourney Weaver:

> You try getting on a bus and reading a book, hoping to disappear and not being able to. There's no way you can know what it's like until you are famous. There are very few reasons why it's worthwhile, and believe me it's not something most actors crave or wholeheartedly enjoy.[42]

It seems extraordinary that both a rock singer and a film star should deny that the recognition of the public is not a major factor behind their desire for success in their chosen field (Vedder uses the word 'success' in a more understated way, presumably synonymous with 'fame'). Vedder's argument that his band were not prepared for success is plausible; however it seems to ignore an important element in the whole process of becoming a rock musician, and one which I believe is at the heart of much of the negative experience of celebrity.

Look again at Vedder's reasons for getting 'into this' – being in a band, playing music, making records. Playing music is, of course, something that human beings have done for several millennia without necessarily becoming famous; many millions of people today 'play music' and remain anonymous. But being 'in a band' and making records are not activities which are performed in private. On the contrary, they are intrinsically public activities, about as exhibitionist and self-publicizing as they come. Very few teenagers form bands without imagining a performance on a raised stage in front of enthusiastic fans. Nobody makes a record without expecting it to copy itself and transport their music to all kinds of people. Vedder's failure to acknowledge that these activities are inseparable from fame and 'success' is by no means unusual, but it suggests that he has unrealistic expectations about the sphere of activity in which he has chosen to operate.

Likewise, Sigourney Weaver's comment that very few actors crave or enjoy fame is highly ironic, given the role that public fame and adulation play in the whole process of film stardom. This ambivalence is captured perfectly in Kenneth Williams's diaries, which include the following entry: 'The staring, the stopping in the street, the nudging of people when they recognize me – my fear of them – my *hate* of them, my desire to get away from their prying eyes...It's the utter loneliness of the existence.'[43] It is a typical set of remarks from a modern celebrity, similar to those reported earlier in the chapter, with all the characteristic features, such as invasion of privacy ('prying eyes') and the ultimate sensation of loneliness. However, in a later part of the diaries, we find this entry:

> I walked to Berman's and in Stanhope Street they were drilling the road and I noticed the blond man handling the pneumatic was v. handsome...then his friend alongside saw me and called out 'Hallo Ken! You're looking well!' and they both chorused greetings to me. I loved it and simpered my 'Thank you very much' like a schoolboy receiving unexpected praise. O! I do adore these kind of men.[44]

It could of course be argued that these entries are simply characteristic of the affected contrariness of their author!

Actors and musicians often make a distinction between their 'art' which they aspire to perfect, and the irksome attention of the public, no matter how talented or critically fêted they are. This can cause considerable problems, most evident when they receive negative press coverage (it was a series of poor reviews which were cited as the reason for the British actor Stephen Fry's temporary disappearance early in 1995). The media usually respond by claiming that if it wasn't for their publicity the stars would be languishing in obscurity, and they are perfectly correct. Nevertheless, it is the belief that they are acting out their innate gifts (a view so often propagated by the media themselves) that drives the celebrities on, even when press and public alike have their thumbs down.

The distinction between the gift and public acclaim is harder to reconcile in sport, and for this reason relations between celebrities and the press are at their worst in this area. The problem with sport is that it is one of the few areas of public life which is truly meritocratic. Sports stars can be seen to excel at their particular craft; they can *prove* they are the best. At the same time, the public – at least, as far as the media is concerned – are interested in more than the visible features of the sporting celebrity. They want to know about sports stars' private lives and any gossip of which they might be the subject. As a result, a sporting celebrity may be beyond criticism in his or her performance, may even be a national hero, and yet receive more press coverage for negative, scandal-related issues. Again there is this conflict between the rights and responsibilities of celebrities: once you have put yourself, for whatever reason, in the public eye, do you not have a responsibility for your behaviour and a duty to your fans to supply them with entertainment away from the sports field? As with pop stars and film stars, the rewards of sporting fame are intimately bound up with the acclaim of the press and public.

Preparing for fame

The celebrity quotes throughout this chapter suggest that, while the rewards of fame are undeniably worthwhile, they are frequently spoiled by a host of associated perils that may combine to produce acute psychological distress and, in some cases, an extreme psychopathological response. It seems that there must be a role psychology can play in the fame process. At present, celebrities call upon mental health professionals when the going gets tough; Princess Diana's use of psychotherapist Susie Orbach is well documented, and many American film stars, such as Jim Carrey, are reported to 'have shrinks'.

Many of the quotes reported here seem to suggest that the psychological difficulties of celebrities result from changes in lifestyle in the early stages of fame. The benefits of fame exert such a pull that there is a tendency for new celebrities to dwell only on the positive aspects of fame, so that the negative aspects arrive unexpectedly and suddenly. The singer Gary Numan's comments below seem to support this theory:

> [Becoming famous] was nothing like I expected it to be...I often equate it to losing your virginity. You think about it forever and when

it happens it is almost an anti-climax. You feel deeply unprepared for it and you really have to learn how to do it.[45]

Clearly there is a need for celebrities to be better prepared for fame, beyond the helpful contributions of financial advisers and the cocooning influence of record companies, football clubs and the like. Such preparation might even extend to the friends and families of the famous, whose role becomes increasingly important as fame exerts its pressures.

Conclusion

This chapter has examined in detail the nature of psychological problems encountered by the famous. The reasons for these problems include the high price afforded to privacy in contemporary Western society, the inability to manage the sudden intrusion of large numbers of new acquaintances, difficulty in balancing the pleasures and irritations of public recognition, and the perpetual gaze of the media. Many of these problems, it is suggested, could perhaps be alleviated by a greater preparedness by celebrities for the negative aspects of fame.

However, in discussing the 'problems' of celebrity, it must be borne in mind that celebrity is not a homogeneous experience, and 'preparedness' is more important in some activities than in others. It is for these reasons that I attempt, in Chapter 7, to construct some form of classification system relating to the way fame is achieved, which might help us understand the specific areas of difficulty experienced by different types of celebrity.

Chapter 7
A taxonomy of fame

At this point it seems apposite to return to some of the concerns of the opening chapter, where I drew a distinction between 'fame' and 'celebrity'. Fame, I argued, is best regarded as the process by which people become well-known. What constitutes well-known-ness? It must surely be defined as a degree of public knowledge above what would be expected of an individual, given his or her social status and the type of relationship network s/he would be expected to have. This definition does not, by itself, account for the fact that, for whatever reason, some individuals are simply more *popular* than others. But fame is a level of well-known-ness beyond what can be achieved through mere popularity, and so it requires either a specific deed or achievement to generate publicity, or a vehicle for the spread of news. I have made this definition of fame sufficiently broad that it might be applied to limited contexts, such as a school or a small geographical area. Celebrity, by contrast, is a phenomenon associated with mass communication, specifically television and print media. All celebrities are famous; for better or worse, most famous people are now celebrities.

Does this mean, then, that Maureen from *Driving School* and Shakespeare are destined to share the same pedestal in the public imagination? Clearly not. The *routes* by which those two individuals arrived at fame are so radically different from each other that to treat them under the same banner of 'general fame' might make this whole project worthless. Clearly there are factors which are common to all people who share the property of celebrity. However, it is necessary to create some means of distinguishing different types of fame, and the different processes which bring about celebrity.

In this chapter I describe how I have gone about breaking down fame into its components, and how my colleagues at Sheffield Hallam University and I have attempted some initial exploration of the theory. The whole model I have called a *taxonomy* (a system of classification derived from biology), which comprises two main parts: a *typology* (what different basic types of fame are there?) and a hierarchy of *levels* (degrees of fame). There is a third element to the taxonomy, and that is a time dimension which I have called the *fame trajectory*. There is also a possible fourth dimension, which may be more related to cognitive processes, concerning the nature of the information which is retained about an individual celebrity. The levels and the trajectory are largely in an embryonic state; however the typology has been tested on a student sample, and the categories appear to be reasonably robust. The results of this study will be described in a later part of the chapter.

The concept of a taxonomy of fame is not a new one. In the nineteenth century, both the American poet and philosopher Ralph Waldo Emerson and the British writer Thomas Carlyle separately attempted to create a typology of famous people (exclusively men) through history.[1] Each typology was based firmly on the individual's sphere of activity. Emerson selected Plato to represent philosophers, Shakespeare to represent poets, and so on, while Carlyle's list of 'heroes' includes prophets (Mohammed) as well as kings and 'men of letters'. The types are not always distinct; for example, Emerson lists poets and writers as separate categories. If nothing else, they represent the activities and attributes which were considered worthy of canonization in the mid-1800s.

However, the system I am proposing here is not so much activity-oriented as, in keeping with the theoretical stance of the book, process-oriented; it is concerned with the ways and means of becoming famous. It is a system which, if not quite allowing Maureen to share a pedestal with Shakespeare, at least enables them to stand on adjacent footstools.[2]

The typology of fame

The basic rationale behind the typology described here is that I have tried to separate, as far as possible, the Braudy-style 'true fame' from the instant fame of the modern celebrity. Therefore, consideration of individual *merit* must play a part (along with the acknowledgement that what constitutes merit will fluctuate both historically and culturally). However, because I am considering fame as a process, there are certain types of famous person who warrant categories of their own because their route to fame is markedly different from others. These are public figures, whose fame is linked to the post they hold in civic life, and, at the other extreme, people who become famous by accident, either through their association with other famous people, or by their involvement in a high-profile news story.

1. Public figures

The first category is reserved for individuals who achieve fame because of their role in society. Two examples would be the President of the United States and the Prime Minister of Britain. The relevance of this category is that fame automatically adheres itself to any individual who holds an office of this kind; it is impervious to personality factors (so a rather colourless individual such as John Major can become hugely famous worldwide), and the job description carries as much significance as the individual's name. The Lord Mayor of London changes identity constantly, the Pope less so. Even if the individual behind the facade is not known by name, the figure of authority retains the fame.

On the face of it, it might seem irreverent to talk of political figures as celebrities. Are these not individuals who are acting on behalf of the people, whose motives for being in the public eye are essentially philanthropic, far removed from the narcissism we usually associate with 'celebrity'? Historically, there is little evidence to justify such reverence. The highly individualistic nature of democratic politics is enough to counter any suggestion that politicians can be treated as exempt from this taxonomy; the word 'ambition' derives from the Latin *ambitio*, meaning to walk around canvassing for votes.[3] Roman politics was inextricably linked with theatre, and it was in the self-presentation of men like Cicero and Pompey that the iconography of fame was mapped out. By the time leaders such as Caligula were in power, politics had been reduced to little more than the individual personalities of the people involved.

At a more localized level, fame can be guaranteed by holding posts of some authority within the community. For example, a local Member of Parliament, the head teacher of a school, or the current president of the British Psychological Society are all famous by virtue of their positions. Again, we may not know their names as individuals; recognition here may be confined to the face. Alternatively we may simply be aware of them as local figures.

Once in the public eye as an authority figure, individuals acquire fame for other deeds, not necessarily related to the roles of office. This is certainly true of Denis Healey, as mentioned earlier in the book, who became best known to the public when caricatured by an impressionist. A contemporary example is David Mellor, the Conservative MP who first attained a certain amount of fame through being a member of Margaret Thatcher's cabinet. He only became a leading celebrity when he was the subject of a lurid sex scandal involving a highly attractive actress and a much-publicized toe-sucking incident. During the scandal it was revealed that Mellor was a devoted football fan (even insisting on wearing the Chelsea strip while making love!) and this soon led to a number of sports-related media engagements. The most recent of these has seen him host a football-related phone-in show on BBC radio.

In making this transition from jobbing politician to radio star, Mellor's fame clearly exceeded that which would usually accompany a minor cabinet post. It is evidence that, once famous via one route, individuals may migrate to other categories of fame through their subsequent activities. Therefore this typology only holds true for any given moment in time, unless we use it to account for an individual's initial rise to prominence.

2. Meritocratic fame

This category comes closest to representing Leo Braudy's ideal of fame, originally derived from honour, where fame was earned through enduring achievement. However I feel we need to be more explicit about the qualities that are actually represented by *meritocratic* fame. The qualification for this category is that an individual has earned fame through merit alone.

The problem for the typology is one of establishing what precisely is meant by merit. Time is a factor; it is hard to venerate someone for today's achievements when they may fade by tomorrow. The examples of Alexander and Jesus are troublesome for the typology because we only have the legends upon which we can base their claims to merit. What one is good at may be highly esoteric, hard to pin down. More importantly still, the norms of the dominant culture at any given time dictate which activities are worthy of recognition. As the twentieth century has progressed, sporting achievement has become increasingly revered in the West, while other activities have declined in popularity. In Greek and Roman times, certain activities were privileged over others: music was highly prized in Ancient Greece to the extent that one was considered 'uneducated' if unmusical, while oratory was more important to Romans. Other activities need to prove their worthiness through durability; it took 30 years for broadsheet newspapers to take pop music seriously. Even when Shakespeare was at his peak, plays were not regarded as serious art forms, being seen as 'too ephemeral and popular to be called "works"'.[4] Indeed, it was not until his later plays that Shakespeare's name actually appeared on the title pages.

One reason for the modern eminence of sport is that its rewards, unlike those of other public activities, are highly visible and *quantifiable*. Linford Christie at his peak was the fastest runner in the world. He had the medals, the record times and the videotapes to prove it. You cannot be a famous footballer without being good at football. Sports such as cricket, which are saturated with statistics, are even more unambiguous; if you score enough runs or take enough wickets you will eventually be picked to represent your country. If you don't you will never rise beyond the ranks of club or county and your opportunities for fame are extremely limited.

Therefore it could be argued that sportspeople are the best examples of category two fame. The water becomes muddier when we move into the arts and sciences, though in the traditional areas of academy-based achievement, there is little doubting the merits of the famous. The most famous scientists are usually either outstanding writers or researchers, or both. Classical music and serious literature are areas where the entry qualifications are extremely high; you cannot, for example, be a famous classical musician without an extensive musical education. The status enjoyed by these fields is another matter entirely. Our reverence for classical musicians and novelists is determined by the cultural traditions of our society, and yet it is harder for these people to achieve fame than in activities of less obvious merit.

Nevertheless, how do we recognize merit in popular culture? Is mere popularity a reliable yardstick? The Beatles and the Spice Girls have each had strings of number one records, but come the year 2010 it is unlikely that they will be seen as equally talented. How about Oasis? It seems that *time* may be a better measure. However, we may disagree profoundly as to the merits of 1970s pop groups.[5]

One suggestion is that artistic change is driven by the need for fame, because fame is often granted through originality (being the *first* to have achieved something), a process which has been termed 'aesthetic evolution'.[6] The argument is that, as an art form settles into a specific pattern of normative values and methods, it becomes increasingly difficult for an individual to stand out, and so there is a natural trend towards original combinations of artistic materials in order to bring about change (and accompanying fame), and in doing so this often results in a complete change of art form. Today, our awareness of the ebb and flow of history may make us unusually respectful of originality – a good example here would be the veneration shown for many modern 'classical' composers, whom we respect as important figures even when we find their music hideously unlistenable. An interesting study relating to aesthetic judgment was carried out by Mustapha Sherif as long ago as 1935, in which participants were asked to evaluate a series of prose passages on the assumption that they were written by famous authors.[7] The results showed a high correlation between participants' order of preference for the passages and their preference for the supposed authors. However, all the passages had been written by the same person.

3. Showbusiness 'stars'

Category three is the one which most closely corresponds to the definition of celebrity. For this we can perhaps adapt Ruth Gledhill's definition of a film star as an actor who is celebrated more for their off-screen lifestyle and personality than for their acting ability.[8] This definition can be applied to celebrities from any field; clearly, 'ability' in some fields (music, for instance) is harder to surpass than ability in others (presenting a television show). In a strongly meritocratic field such as sport, it is unusual for an individual to be celebrated for something other than their sporting ability, though it does happen (Eddie Edwards, for instance).

It could be argued that membership of this category is also dependent on whether the individual has set out 'to be famous' at any cost, rather than performing an activity and receiving fame as a by-product. However, as suggested in Chapter 1, fame is much less a by-product of some activities (for example, pop or film stardom) than others (for example, academia). Clearly there is a vast 'grey area' between categories two and three which may need time, and possibly shifts in mainstream culture, to resolve. Indeed, it is probably fair to say that the majority of individuals in category three would argue for inclusion in category two, however slender their case.

4. Accidental fame

In some respects, this category is thoroughly contemporary, peopled by individuals who have achieved fame through notoriety, or through public access media of some kind. However, myths and legends have not always centred around willing subjects; criminals and their victims have long been the topic of newspaper headlines, and fame has often attached itself to the most unfortunate recipients.

Nevertheless it is easier to become famous today than ever before – more outlets, less talent required – and so it could be argued that the numbers in this category have swelled disproportionately over the last 20 years. Typical examples include Maureen Reece and Paul Nolan (see Chapter 1). In these two cases, fame's spotlight sought out these individuals, regardless of their intentions; however much they may have milked their celebrity status subsequently, they remain members of category four until they become Prime Minister, win an Olympic medal or release a string of successful singles.

It is worth noting though, that just because an individual has achieved fame through a vehicle like a fly-on-the-wall TV documentary, this does not mean to say that their fame is truly accidental. A case in point is Jane McDonald, a singer who achieved instant success after her appearance on a BBC documentary about a cruise liner (*The Cruise*). Her 'break' was purely accidental; but she had been searching for success for many years previously. If we were to include McDonald in category four we would have to include all those who enjoyed a degree of luck at some critical point in their career, which would probably not leave us much in the way of a typology (even meritocratic celebrities, it could be argued, need a certain amount of luck at some stage).

Another group of individuals who must be included in this category are those who achieve fame *by association* – because they accidentally become involved in a major story in conjunction with an established celebrity, or because they have an association with a celebrity that bestows fame on them automatically – for example, as the long-standing partner of a political figure. A classic example of the first kind would be Monica Lewinsky, or Christine Keeler (whose affair with cabinet minister John Profumo was a factor in the downfall of the Conservative government in the early 1960s). Publicist Max Clifford has claimed that, from his professional point of view, this type of fame is the quickest and easiest to achieve.[9] Much PR work involves linking sexually receptive celebrities, thus ensuring maximum publicity for both; of course, for this to happen the individuals in question must satisfy certain essential criteria (sexual attractiveness, for example!).

This type of fame has a long history as well; one example is Hans Holbein, the painter whose name has been associated through history with that of Henry VIII, whose portrait he painted.[10] As the publishing industry flourished, the same could be said of editors, translators and, eventually, critics, who earned their reputation on the back of others' loftier achievements .

Levels of fame

This next part of the taxonomy recognizes the fact that fame, as a process, exists independently of the mass media (which have dominated my description of the four types). Even more than the types, the levels are only relevant in a given time period, and an individual can only truly 'belong' to the highest level at which s/he is famous. However it would not be true to say that fame develops in the same way for all individuals. Many may start off at level one or two and progress steadily upwards, but many enter at level three. These anomalies can only be explained by a consideration of type; the path of fame differs according to the nature of the activity.

1. Domain-specific fame

Achievement within a specific domain may only be sufficient for fame within that domain. This is particularly true of 'academic stardom',[11] where fame brings high rewards within academia, and may even produce diminishing returns if it spreads any wider (such as the loss of 'credibility', or the perceived loss of integrity). A scientist writing an influential book or paper (for example, Stephen Hawking) will begin his or her path to fame at this level. Similarly, sports stars necessarily begin at this level, since they will be well-known only to connoisseurs until they reach international competition, and then only to the general public when they do something which attracts the attention of the mainstream media (for example, a footballer starring in the World Cup, or having a romantic liaison with another celebrity).

2. Fame in the local community

This level represents fame which is constrained, either geographically or institutionally. Some people may attain considerable fame within the local regional community, such as a local politician, or radio presenter, without that fame spreading any wider. Alternatively, fame may be restricted within a particular establishment or institution, such as a university or school – for example, my fellow primary-school pupil Parrish, described in Chapter 1. There is a slight overlap between levels one and two in that domain-specific fame can leak out into the local community; for example, academics often get featured in the local press. Alternatively, local and domain fame may co-exist. In the Hillsborough district of Sheffield, there is a pork butcher named Freddie Funk, who would be famous locally for his name alone were it not for his expertise in making pies and sausages, for which he frequently wins national awards (the actor Michael Palin, a native of Sheffield, has been seen in his shop). Likewise, a music teacher at my primary school (again) was well-known locally for his international success at the board game 'Go' – an overlap between two communities (local and school) and one domain!

3. National fame

How could national fame be measured? One (somewhat laborious) way would be to combine the frequency of mention in print media with the frequency of mention, and appearance, on television. Even then we would be assuming that, if an individual is talked about within the media they will automatically be talked about by the public. An alternative way would be to present a large and varied sample of the general public with a list of names and ask which were familiar. Even then we might have to probe further, asking for details of what each celebrity did, or how they knew about them.

Nevertheless, national fame – as a concept – could be described as mass media recognition. We must be careful to control for high-visibility *domain* fame, such as that of sports performers, since that is still domain-*specific*; the difference between the fame of, say, the England cricketer Angus Fraser and the pork butcher Freddie Funk is that, unless I am mistaken, cricket boasts rather more connoisseurs than pork butchery.

4. International fame

This is the hardest of all the levels to ascertain, although the methods suggested for level three could be adapted for a cross-section of different nations. How does an individual progress from level three to level four? Again the answer rests with the mass media, and is partly determined by celebrity type.

Category one fame really depends on the prominence of role; the queen is internationally famous largely for historical reasons, and the president of the United States is guaranteed international fame as a result of contemporary power structures. But few people outside the Middle East would normally be familiar with the name of the president of Iraq; to achieve international fame from such a source requires a major intervention in world politics. Lesser office-holders, such as British cabinet ministers, are unlikely to achieve world fame unless they are implicated in newsworthy political developments. One example of this would be the Australian MP Pauline Hanson, or French right-wing politician Jean-Marie Le Pen, who have attracted fame beyond their countries for their controversial political views.

Category two (meritocratic) and three (showbusiness) individuals require a degree of cultural homogeneity for their names to be famous beyond their own countries or cultures. The name of Ian Botham would be recognized by most British people but by very few people in non-cricket-playing nations. Footballers, however, can achieve worldwide fame (with the exception of the United States!) with relative ease, especially for their exploits in the World Cup. Although their cultural appeal would appear to be quite specific, Western film stars and pop stars have attracted worldwide fame since the 1960s. Predicting overseas success has always proved difficult. Frequently certain acts achieve more success beyond their own country of origin. During the 1980s, British band A Flock of Seagulls had considerable success in the US when they were relatively obscure in Britain, and never really achieved recognition in their country of origin. More recently, the British rock band Bush has achieved worldwide success without selling many records back home.

How do category four (accidental fame) individuals receive international fame? The answer is similar to the way they achieve national fame – as a result of the mass media taking a particular interest in a news story. Individuals such as Maureen Reece are unlikely to become famous beyond Britain because their fame is so closely tied to a specific television programme and the media coverage surrounding that programme (*Driving School* may yet be sold overseas, but without the accompanying media it is unlikely to result in the same degree of stardom!).

Fame trajectories

Fame trajectories are the third dimension of fame. For an individual they could be mapped out in terms of media coverage (mentions in the press, appearances on television) and might be expected to show a pattern consistent with his or her type and level of fame. This is the dimension most amenable to quantitative research. Keith Simonton has produced career trajectories for scientists based on career 'landmarks', such as significant publications, which demonstrate distinct patterns across disciplines.[12] Similar trajectories might be developed for different sports, or branches of the arts, or specific combinations of fame type and level. These could be used to predict possible psychological effects of national-level fame (such as a 'honeymoon period' where the benefits of fame initially outweigh the negative aspects or, alternatively, a period of declining fame typically experienced after career landmarks).

For example, a scientist's career trajectory is more than likely to have something approaching a normal distribution. Typically, a scientist's first work is produced in his or her late 20s or early 30s (though this seems to be based on academic publication, a notoriously fickle guide); their 'best' work at around 40, and the last in their mid-50s. A fame trajectory, based on something like the frequency of mention outside academia (in the media, perhaps) would almost certainly have a skew to the right-hand side, since achievement tends to lag somewhat behind fame for academics (Einstein being a classic example). Alternatively, there are few catwalk models aged over 30, so a typical model will have a fame trajectory which is skewed to the left.

Memorable characteristics of famous people

A fourth dimension to the taxonomy refers to the information which is retained about famous individuals. Before the advent of portraiture, it was largely a person's *name* that carried their fame, and much of the early literature on the subject refers to people achieving posterity either through the written word or through the 'lips' of gossip and story-telling. In today's highly visual culture it is likely that *faces* are more important aspects of famous people, although there are some types/levels in which names are still fame's currency – in academia, for example, where we can know an individual's work and reputation intimately, but have never clapped eyes on him or her. It may be that there are a large number of people within a given culture for whom the opposite is true – their faces are recognized instantly, and yet we are unable to supply any further

Table 7.1 Types and levels of fame, with examples

Types of fame	Levels of fame			
	Domain-specific (e.g., psychology)	Community-based	National	International
1. Public figures	BPS president	Local MP	Jack Straw (British Home Secretary)	Bill Clinton
2. Meritocratic	Winner of an academic award?	Freddie Funk	Kate Adie (BBC foreign affairs correspondent)	Linford Christie
3. Showbusiness 'stars'	Raj Persaud (TV psychiatrist)	Parrish?	Chris Evans (DJ and TV presenter)	Hugh Grant
4. Accidental	'Little Albert'	One of Parrish's victims?	Maureen Reece	Divine Brown

information. This might be the case where people are famous through their role in advertisements or as photographic models. Table 7.1 above displays an attempt to generate examples of individuals who belong to each of the types and levels of the taxonomy.

A test of the typology

A relatively simple way of testing the robustness of the four types of fame is to ask one group of people to generate names for each category and another group to say if they agree. If the first part of the exercise is achievable – and has some internal consistency – this in itself suggests that the categories are meaningful.

The participants in our study were the current first- and second-year undergraduates at Sheffield Hallam University. Like so many studies in psychology it can be criticized for its use of the nearest available subject pool (that is, the researchers' students!). I shall not attempt to claim, then, that our participants are in any way typical of the general population; indeed, their overall youth may mean that they are astute consumers of popular culture and may have a better grasp of contemporary celebrity than most, which may make them ideal candidates for this type of exercise. It must also be borne in mind that the vast majority of respondents were female, which may or may not account for their choice of nominations (and maybe for their category judgements).

Stage 1

Data was collected in two stages. The first stage required participants to generate at least four examples of each celebrity type, on the basis of the following information:

1. *Public figures*. Famous mainly because of the professional role s/he plays in society.
2. *Famous on merit*. Famous mainly because s/he is exceptionally good in her or his chosen field.
3. *Showbusiness 'stars'*. Famous mainly because s/he works in a field which places them directly in the public eye.

4. *Accidental 'stars'*. Famous mainly as a result of forces beyond his or her control.

38 second-year undergraduates completed the questionnaire, generating a total of 577 names. 156 names were generated for category one, 150 for category two, 152 for category three, and 119 for category four. These figures suggest that, although the respondents had no difficulty each generating four examples for the first three categories, they were only able to generate three examples on average for category four. This does not in itself pose a problem for the typology, since one might expect 'accidental stars' to be a smaller category than the others. Of the 577 total names, 214 specific celebrities were named at least once; the most frequently cited names, along with the categories for which they were generated, are listed in Table 7.2.

These data suggest that the categories themselves appear reasonably robust, the majority of citations falling into one category only. Two exceptions to this rule, however, are David Beckham who straddles categories two and three, and, more interestingly, Prince Charles, 40 per cent of whose citations place him in category four. This might be an indicator of public sympathy for the Royal Family (Prince William appeared four times,

Table 7.2 *Frequency of mention for the twelve most popular celebrity names by category*

Name	Categories/Types of fame				
	1	2	3	4	Total
Tony Blair	33	1	0	0	34
The Queen	21	0	0	0	21
Louise Woodward	0	0	0	19	19
Bill Clinton	17	0	0	0	17
Maureen Reece	0	0	0	13	13
Margaret Thatcher	11	1	0	0	12
Madonna	0	0	11	0	11
Chris Evans	0	1	10	0	11
David Beckham	0	8	3	0	11
Richard Branson	7	3	0	0	10
John Major	10	0	0	0	10
Prince Charles	6	0	0	4	10

each in category four); however the Queen is unequivocally a 'public figure'.

Stage 2

37 celebrities were cited at least four times in Stage 1, and it was decided to use these names as the basis for the main study. A table was designed which contained each celebrity name alongside four boxes corresponding to each category. Participants were asked to indicate, in each box, to what extent they agreed with the following statements, by writing a number from 1 (strongly disagree) to 10 (strongly agree):

1. *Public figures*. I know this person mainly because of the professional role s/he plays in society.
2. *Famous on merit*. I know this person mainly because s/he is exceptionally good in his or her chosen field.
3. *Showbusiness 'stars'*. I know this person mainly because s/he works in a field which places him or her directly in the public eye.
4. *Accidental 'stars'*. I know this person mainly because s/he is famous as a result of forces beyond his or her control.

The questionnaire was completed by 160 first-year undergraduates.

The mode responses for the four categories for each celebrity are displayed in Table 7.3. The mode was chosen as a more reliable measure of central tendency than the mean, partly because a sizeable minority misunderstood the point of the exercise and the mode ignores their responses. For example, one respondent surrounded David Beckham's name with kisses and hearts and awarded him 10 for each category; and another awarded Divine Brown (the prostitute who was on the point of administering oral sex to Hugh Grant when arrested) a score of seven in category two (although a more discerning respondent simply wrote 'ask Hugh'!).

It could be argued that ignoring the means in this way is an attempt to cover up a botched exercise, with no consistency of response. Therefore, to alleviate any doubts about the reliability of the approach, a column has been included in the table which contains the frequency of the highest mode response (thus demonstrating consistency among the sample).

Table 7.3 *Mode rating for each category for the 38 celebrities (and frequency of the highest category mode value for each celebrity)*

Name	Frequency of highest mode value	Mode value for each category			
		1	2	3	4
Bill Clinton	71	10	8	1	1
William Hague	68	10	5	1	1
Trevor Rees-Jones	67	1	1	1	10
David Beckham	66	1	10	1	1
The Queen	63	10	1	1	1
Tom Cruise	59	3	8	10	1
Michael Jackson	59	1	7	10	1
Madonna	59	1	6	10	1
George Clooney	58	1	1	10	1
Louise Woodward	57	1	1	1	10
Mo Mowlam	57	10	1	1	1
Tony Blair	56	10	8	1	1
Robert De Niro	56	1	7	10	1
Bruce Forsyth	55	1	1	10	1
Margaret Thatcher	54	10	8	1	1
Liam Gallagher	53	1	1	9	1
Tim Henman	51	1	10	1	1
Maureen Reece	51	1	1	2	8
Linford Christie	50	1	10	1	1
John Major	49	7	7	2	1
Johnny Vaughan	49	1	1	10	1
Terry Waite	49	1	9	2	10
Leonardo Di Caprio	47	1	1	10	1
Cilla Black	46	1	1	8	1
Divine Brown	46	1	1	2	8
Cherie Blair	45	6	1	1	4
Richard Branson	44	7	8	1	1
Prince Charles	44	8	1	1	9
Eddie Edwards	44	1	1	1	8
Mother Theresa	44	1	8	1	1
Jim Carrey	43	1	1	8	1
Chris Evans	43	1	5	8	1
Trevor McDonald	43	1	5	7	1
Celine Dion	41	1	1	9	2
Nelson Mandela	41	10	9	1	1
Kate Adie	40	1	6	5	1
Princess Diana	39	10	8	1	1

The data in table 7.3 provide further evidence for the robustness of the categories, with most celebrities attaining a mode of 10 in one specific category. Furthermore, the mode for 32 of the celebrities fell into the category in which the name had originally been generated. Again, a number of celebrities straddled two categories: royal figures other than the Queen, who have high responses in categories one and four; media workers such as Trevor McDonald and Kate Adie; and miscellaneous international figures such as Nelson Mandela and Princess Diana, attracting high 'merit' ratings but who are also acknowledged as public figures.

Uses of the taxonomy

So, is the typology any good? That remains to be seen. The most important thing is that it is there, has been shown to be largely robust, and can now be used as a framework for future research. Such research might involve an investigation into the psychological effects of fame that are peculiar to each category. For public figures, for example, intrusion into privacy might be the most distressing aspect of fame (partly because it may detract from the seriousness of their work). For showbusiness stars, however, it might be that the fear of stalkers and random assault is more important. We would expect accidental stars to be the most ill-prepared to handle fame (since they are the ones who least expect it), although this may also be difficult for many meritocratic stars, who are more focused on achievement than on fame *per se*.

As far as the taxonomy as a whole is concerned, there would need to be large-scale collection of data which can be used to support the levels of fame and the trajectories associated with the various combinations of type and level. An index of fame would need to be established in order to perform this research, such as: number of televised appearances; frequency of citation in newspapers; frequency (and size?) of press photographs; frequency of mention on television. The breadth of the mass media would make such a task immense, so a meaningful hierarchy would need to be identified, both at national and international levels.

How might society benefit from this research? As I have tried to argue in the remainder of this book, fame is not a subject to be taken lightly – it affects our lives more than we may acknowledge, and it certainly affects the lives of those who have become famous, without any obvious benefit apart from wealth. They are an important sector of society who have been neglected by social science in general, perhaps because they are seen as less deserving of attention (being rich), and perhaps because their experiences seem so bound up with the machinations of the media that we sometimes forget that they exist away from the silver screen.

Conclusions

The main focus of this chapter has been the rationale for, and testing of, an original taxonomy of fame, comprising a typology of four categories of famous individual and four levels of fame, with dimensions of time and information underpinning the model. This is by no means intended to be a definitive model; other taxonomies might serve more useful research purposes, but I have intended it to remain fairly true to the concept of fame as a process. The typology, for example, might be widened considerably to allow for specific routes to fame (professional sport, for instance, or fashion modelling). There would of course need to be some conceptual basis for such classifications. Furthermore, the existing taxonomy could be subjected to much more rigorous testing; for example, by using a specially designed list of celebrity names and performing some form of cluster analysis or, perhaps, by using a Q-sort technique through which participants could generate their own categorical system.

Chapter 8

Beyond parasocial interaction: fans and stalkers

At this point I shall return to the subject matter of Chapter 4, in which I discussed the phenomenon of parasocial relationships. To recap, these are relationships formed between viewers and celebrities (or anyone who appears on the television), in which interaction seems to be unilateral, and it could be argued that they are not 'relationships' at all. Such an argument rests on the assumption that the interaction between viewer and celebrity is permanently confined to the viewer's uses and gratifications of the medium.

There is, however, a sense in which these relationships are not truly *para*social at all. Parasocial interaction is an accurate way of describing relationships formed with mythical beings, say, cartoon figures, or *characters* in drama (as opposed to the actors who play them). These 'relationships' are illusory, however meaningful they may be (especially for children), because they can never be more than unilateral – internal, private relationships affecting only the viewer. However, when we form a parasocial relationship with a celebrity – a pop star for example – we are, effectively, entering into a relationship with a living being with whom a bilateral relationship is a possibility. Furthermore, the term 'parasocial interaction' hardly does justice to the kind of relationship radio listeners have with celebrity broadcasters, who often devote a section of their show to telephone conversation with members of the public.

The more we wish to enter into a relationship with a specific celebrity, the more we seem likely to do so. As opportunities increase for the public to become famous, so do opportunities for other points of contact between celebrities and the public.

Celebrities do more than open fêtes. They frequently visit schools and hospitals; they often take part themselves in public access media – for example, taking part in a 'phone-in' (a series of telephone interviews with the public, particularly on Saturday morning children's television); often special arrangements are made for celebrities to meet certain members of the public. In Japan there is a very well-established structure of support groups (*koenkai*), or fan clubs, which play an important commercial (promotional) role in the careers of celebrities. Sometimes these organize events where fans can meet their idols and even take part in a 'telephone date' with them. [1]

In this chapter, I discuss what happens when public interaction with celebrities goes beyond the parasocial – when the famous are forced to take notice of us, even though we are no more than one of the anonymous millions. I will examine the phenomenon of *fandom* – where members of the public idolize one special celebrity, often to the point of obsession, and the psychological significance of this obsession for both the fan and the celebrity involved. Obsessive fandom has its more disturbing manifestation, celebrity stalking, and there have been an increasing number of incidents in recent years where celebrities have been assaulted (or even, in certain cases, killed) by obsessed fans. What role might fandom play in modern society? Are there any historical precedents? The answers to these questions may prove elusive, but they are crucial to understanding the function of fandom.

Fans

The origins of fandom stretch as far back as the origins of fame. Alexander the Great was, of course, the first celebrated example of a fan, except his heroes were the stuff of legends. Those who followed Alexander in later generations were his fans, although he was not around to 'interact' with them. Because fame in earlier times did not have the rapid communication vehicles of later media, one's fame would take longer to reach the public than today. Nevertheless Jesus had his fair share of fans (modern fans are still referred to as 'disciples'). It was really not until the Middle Ages that fans reappeared though, hounding Petrarch with their poems as he travelled across

Europe, and with the birth of mass communication in the eighteenth century.

Rousseau in particular was tormented by the attentions of fans.[2] People would travel hundreds of miles to see him, even if they were uninterested in literature and had not read his work. After a while he began to imagine they were spies sent by governments who disapproved of his political views. The most famous early fan of all was the writer James Boswell, who is largely remembered for his project to turn his idol – Samuel Johnson – into a superstar. He hoped his *Life of Johnson* would enable his hero to be seen 'more completely than any man who has ever yet lived'. It is at this point, argues Leo Braudy, that fandom emerged in its modern-day form, as the audience of fame 'takes an active role in defining [its idols]'.[3]

The word *fan* has clear religious origins. The Latin *fanaticus* (literally, 'belonging to the temple') gradually acquired a more negative connotation, indicating inappropriate or erroneous enthusiasm, usually for a disapproved activity. The first recorded use of the shortened version ('fan') appeared in nineteenth-century sports journalism in the United States, and was adopted by theatre critics, who used it disapprovingly to refer to the trend among (mostly female) theatre-goers who were beginning to prize actors over the plays themselves (paving the way for the 'film star' explosion in Hollywood in the following century).[4]

Much of the recent work on fandom has examined the phenomenon from the 'active audience' perspective. Joshua Gamson distinguishes the modern celebrity fan from the earlier, pre-war variety, by a change in attitude towards the 'artificiality' of stars.[5] He regards fandom as primarily a social activity (rather than private interaction), although he is largely concerned with what he calls 'celebrity watchers', who have a generic interest in famous individuals rather than an interest in one specific celebrity. However he makes some interesting points about the 'postmodern' fan, who is as interested in the 'game playing' aspect of fandom as in the intense degrees of identification, fantasy and modelling reported by Hollywood fans.

Modern fans, Gamson argues, are highly aware of all the tricks and gimmicks of the celebrity industry, and part of the pleasure of fandom is watching the way the strings are pulled: 'Through irony... celebrity texts position their readers, enlightened about the falseness of celebrity, to "see the joke" of the performed self.'[6] How effective the gimmickry is depends on the skill of the manipulation. Gamson quotes a fan of mother-and-daughter country-and-western outfit the Judds as saying how she was getting increasingly irritated by the hype surrounding the Judds' supposed break-up. It was OK for a couple of months, she says, but by five months, when a 'pay-per-view' TV spectacular had been promoted on the assertion that it was the duo's swansong, it was 'totally taking advantage... pushing the limits of decency'.[7]

An important reference on the subject of fandom is Henry Jenkins's *Textual Poachers*, which stresses the active role of the fan in reappropriating cultural material.[8] Jenkins is primarily concerned with what he terms 'media fans', who are devotees of a single television programme (rather than a specific celebrity). He is strongly critical of the 'pathologizing' portrayal of media fans by both the media itself and the writing of academic researchers.[9] He cites as an example an extraordinary television show in which William Shatner ('Captain Kirk' in the science-fiction series *Star Trek*) confronted an audience of *Star Trek* fans (contemptuously referred to as 'Trekkies'), who wanted him to regale them with all manner of trivial detail concerning specific episodes of the show. In desperation, Shatner rounded on them, exhorting them to 'get a life', accusing them of being socially inadequate. When Shatner stormed off the set, the frantic producer sent him back on again, to pacify the distraught audience by claiming that he had been re-enacting a scene from a specific episode of the show in which Kirk was possessed by an evil spirit!

What Shatner, and the media in general, fail to appreciate, according to Jenkins, is that 'Trekkies' and other 'obsessive' fans are '[turning] the experience of watching television into a rich and complex participatory culture'.[10] It is the passive viewers who are the real losers, wasting away in front of the box. Media fans are 'active readers' (or 'poachers') who reinterpret media texts in order to gain ownership. He quotes from media fans such as a group of 'Trekkies' who meet regularly to watch episodes of the show, to adapt storylines to suit their favourite character and even generate scripts of their own. As support for his argument, Jenkins points to the attempts by corporate bodies to suppress the activities of fan groups, such as the corporately run *Star Wars* fan club attacking 'unofficial' publications for 'violating the family values' promoted in the film. Other examples of textual poaching include gay *Star Trek* fan groups who have spliced video footage of scenes involving Kirk and Spock to create a homosexual love story, and have also produced 'erotic' texts describing in great detail sexual encounters between the two characters.

Although Gamson and Jenkins create convincing arguments, it could be argued that each is concentrating on a very specific type of fan. Jenkins's textual poachers share many of the characteristics of the celebrities who, as I have mentioned on several occasions, start life as fans and become famous through emulating the deeds or styles of their heroes. Particularly in popular music, where there is such importance attached to 'musical influences' and where so much past culture is 'poached' or reinterpreted, this type of fandom is regarded as an essential part of the creative process. Gamson's 'celebrity watchers', while interesting as a subgroup of fans, are quite different to the fans of individual celebrities. Furthermore, his claim that modern media consumers are sophisticated ironists is open to considerable doubt, particularly when seen in the light of the passive soap opera viewer who confronts an actor in public and accuses them of the misdeeds of their fictional character. Such instances are far from unusual: an actress from the BBC soap *EastEnders* recently told the audience of the chat show *Kilroy* how she had hailed a taxi a few days earlier and been given a stern ticking-off by the driver, showing no signs of irony, for her recent behaviour in the show![11]

What distinguishes the true fan from the mere enthusiast? Of course one can be a fan of soul music, a fan of Sheffield Wednesday football club, or a fan of motor sports. These may be more than enthusiasms; they may occupy a central role in one's life, command time and attention that encroaches on one's working life and interferes with close relationships. But enthusiasms for spheres of activity can flourish into occupations or careers, and may involve the enthusiast in much more than a passive capacity. A fan of soul music may end up working as a DJ; a fan of motor sports may eventually take part in them. But celebrity fans are fans of nothing more than a single individual; it is that person who occupies the central role in their life and commands more time, attention and devotion than most people lavish on a romantic partner.

During the 1980s I worked on a teenage 'glossy' pop music magazine called *Number One*, which ran a series of interviews with what we called 'Super Fans'. These were almost invariably teenage girls (who constituted the vast majority of the readership), although the occasional adult made an appearance. I conducted some of these interviews and found the fans themselves to be remarkably ordinary teenagers with sunny dispositions and active social lives, who were proud of their allegiance to a specific star. A Boy George fan estimated that there were 11 714 replications of her idol in her possession – pictures, posters, badges, photographs – and that she spent up to £100 each week on magazines and clothes from the Boy shop (Boy George's retail venture). A Madonna fan had amassed 379 of her heroine's records and filled her bedroom with related merchandise such as 18 T-shirts, mirrors, pillowcases, flags and bags.

These fans were mainly between 16 and 18 years old; many were working and could afford to spend vast sums of money on their obsessions. Most importantly, they had all come close to their idols: even the Madonna fan had been to all four of her London performances the previous year. A Morrissey fan had been touched on the hand. The Boy George fan had actually spoken to him. While their relationships with their idols were hugely one-sided, they were no longer parasocial – although I got the general impression throughout the interviews that, somehow, forging closer relationships with the celebrities was not an ultimate goal. They were quite content to remain distant fans. It was almost as though the celebrity was worshipped for what s/he *represents*, rather than his or her individual personality, even when the attraction had overtly sexual origins.

Why should these activities be primarily the preserve of teenage girls and young women? An interesting perspective is presented in a paper by the journalist and author Sheryl Garratt, who recalls her 1970s interest in the Bay City Rollers and reinterprets this in the light of adulthood, asking the question: 'Why do adolescent girls go loopy over gawky, sometimes talentless young men?'[12] Her explanation is similar to Gamson's: the important feature of fandom is the shared experience, particularly for teenage girls (struggling with real relationships with boys). 'Our real obsession was with ourselves: in the end, the actual men behind the posters had very little to do with it.'[13]

However, Garratt also argues that 'the illusion of accessibility is essential'.[14] The important distinction between teenage boys and girls, she claims, is that while boys have a more realistic chance of attaining fame by themselves, girls are more likely to resign themselves to fame by association – as a star's partner: 'My favourite daydream in school was of a famous star suddenly walking into the room to take me away, leaving my classmates sighing in regret that they hadn't realized I was so wonderful.'[15] This may, of course, be less true today than in the 1970s, with a larger number of famous female role models for girls to choose from, but it demonstrates the way in which fans may use their idols as important tools for identity construction. This point is made clear in Nick Hornby's classic study of football fandom, *Fever Pitch*, in which the author attempts to account for his personal obsession with Arsenal football club:

> You know that on nights like the '89 championship night, or on afternoons like the afternoon of the 1992 Wrexham disaster, you are in the thoughts of scores, maybe even hundreds, of people... old girlfriends and other people you have lost touch with and will probably never see again are sitting in front of their TV sets and thinking, momentarily but *all at the same time*, Nick, just that, and are happy or sad for me.[16]

Maybe fandom is, sometimes, little more than basking in someone else's reflected glory.

Religious parallels

Garratt's interpretation of teenage obsessions contains much valuable insight, but it fails to account for truly obsessive fandom. Out of all the fans interviewed in *Number One*, the Boy George fan had taken her interest the furthest. She had stopped buying records made by other artists ('No one else can compete with him.'). She and her friends had moved near to London so that they could be near their hero, often making pilgrimages to his house, and had renounced their former friends: 'We all moved away from our school friends and things like that, and now I don't think I've got any friends that aren't Boy George fans.' This is more like the entry into a religious cult than a passing teenage 'phase'. It reinforces the impression that the celebrity involved is merely a conduit for some 'higher' entity, though in a secular culture this is not constructed as divine.

Henry Jenkins reports some research conducted by Jewett and Lawrence on what was then a recent emergence of *Star Trek* fans.[17] The researchers concluded that this was 'a strange electronic religion... in the making', and that the publications of fan groups were 'written in the spirit of... religious devotion'. For Jenkins, this is a typically 'pathologizing', and 'absurdly literal' account of fandom by academics, but this may be largely due to its disapproving and incredulous tone. There is nothing intrinsically pathologizing about comparing media fans to religious devotees, since in both instances the roots of devotion are remarkably similar, and the texts produced by *Star Trek* fans and the like (and even some of the more exuberant rock criticism) are not unlike the religious texts of the Middle Ages, which had a similar degree of reinterpretation (of, say, the Gospels) and turned the authors and translators into famous figures, often drawing attention away from the spiritual content of the work they were analysing.[18]

Indeed, there are many elements of *Star Trek* fandom which are deeply religious in nature, as detailed in a remarkable paper by the anthropologist Michael Jindra.[19] Jindra argues that *Star Trek* fandom could be classed as a 'civil' religion (like, for example, L. Ron Hubbard's Church of Scientology). It contains several essential ingredients: an organization (the official fan club); dogmas (the need to maintain consistency in fan literature relating to the films or TV series – there is even a *Star Trek* 'canon'); and a form of recruitment system. Furthermore, many fans quoted in Jindra's paper draw their own explicitly religious analogies ('things are not unlike a religion round here'). Most notable of all is the description of a 'ceremony' which took place at a *Star Trek* convention, in which a young child was 'baptized' into a 'Temple of Trek'!

At this point it might be appropriate to return to the Kalasis of Orissa described by Much and Mahapatra which I discussed in Chapter 6. These are people who are 'possessed' by gods at specific times and command a standing in their community far beyond their normal social rank. I argued that similar things happen when people become celebrities in secular cultures. One clear parallel is in the way people react to celebrities when they meet them, and particularly the allowances we make for certain types of behaviour.

At one point in Much and Mahapatra's paper, Nancy Much describes how the Kalasi may beat her supplicants with a cane. 'As she walks to the outside [of the temple] she sometimes whacks a male supplicant with the *beta* (cane). This is not in anger but is taken as a blessing. The man, smiling, bows his head and shoulders and cowers a bit.'[20] It would be stretching credulity to say that this is equivalent to the passive acceptance of bad behaviour by Western celebrities, but the social effects are none the less spectacular.

In the early 1980s Nick Cave, then the singer with Australian rock band, The Birthday Party, would frequently kick the front row of the audience when the band performed live. If a member of the security staff performed the same act, one might expect the audience to pile on to the stage and start a riot; if a member of the audience got on to the stage and kicked spectators he would probably be violently attacked. But the front row of Nick Cave's supplicants took their punishment and wore the bruises proudly afterwards.

A few years earlier, the English football club Nottingham Forest were playing at home at a time when a spate of hooligan incidents had been creating something of a 'moral panic'. They were managed at this time by Brian Clough, a lovable eccentric who was renowned for expressing outrageous points of view. At one point in the match, the pitch was invaded by a number of spectators, one of whom was wearing a clown outfit. Outraged by what he saw as yet another act of mindless hooliganism, Clough himself ran on to the field, singled out the clown, and cuffed him around the head. Not surprisingly, the incident attracted a great deal of media attention, and it subsequently turned out that the 'clown' was a regular Forest supporter and apologized to Clough. The two men were finally united in front of the television cameras and Clough even demonstrated his forgiveness by planting a kiss on the other's cheek!

I mention these two incidents because I feel they contain elements which are not dissimilar to the cowed submissiveness of the Kalasi's supplicants. Because we regard celebrities as 'special people' we are prepared to tolerate personal slights and even acts of violence that we would frequently answer with violence were they performed by members of the public. This is even more true of the media, who in their desperation to interview and picture celebrities, will suffer all manner of indignities. There is a long history of physical assaults by celebrities on members of the press, from Michael Hutchence's altercations with paparazzi to the more private disputes with individual interviewers. There is a tradition in the music industry for interviewers who are perceived to stray beyond the bounds of respectfulness to get the odd clip round the ear from the dignitary on the other side of the tape recorder. Yet these altercations never develop into full-blown fistfights as they might in other contexts; the journalist, once stung, always retreats into his or her shell, knowing that s/he will have the last laugh when s/he comes to write up the piece. Photographers are less fortunate, but the star's record company or management will always arrange to pay for the damage to prevent any legal action from cluttering up their employee's busy schedule.

Why the kid gloves? The answer is that celebrities are the lifeblood of the media, the two co-existing in a kind of twisted symbiosis, typified by the 'build 'em up and knock 'em down' cliché. The popular music press relationship with the stars is permanently on a knife-edge: having puffed an artist or band up to the giddy heights they fear that any subsequent criticism is liable to result in a readers' backlash and falling sales. Most celebrities actually get an easy critical ride as a result. The problem for the journalists is that, in the majority of cases, their readers' loyalty lies less with the publication than with a single band or artist. As evidenced by the 'Super Fans', this loyalty can take them to extreme lengths, even in the more male-dominated readership of weekly music broadsheets such as *NME* and *Melody Maker*.

To understand fully the parallels between religious belief and fandom it is necessary to examine the things fans say about celebrities. A rich source of material is the work of Fred and Judy Vermorel, who amassed a substantial range of anecdotes, fan letters and interviews which capture some of fandom's greatest excesses (although this work has been criticized by Jenkins for further contributing to the pathologization of fandom). One theme of the Vermorels' research is that of the celebrity as a guardian angel who is constantly watching over the fan. A fan of the 1980s pop group Duran Duran had singled out keyboard player Nick Rhodes for this role, and the following quote is strikingly similar to the comments often made by devout Christians about Jesus Christ (or of religious believers in general about God):

> In these pictures it's like he's looking at you. And that's how I imagine it usually – that he's there and he's looking at me and he can see me and hear me through the magazine... When I stare at one picture for a long time... he's come alive and he's watching me, and he can see and he can move. So I imagine he's here with me all the time and he's watching me all the time. So if I do something I'm careful, because Nick Rhodes is watching me.[21]

A Barry Manilow fan makes the same point, but this time explicitly making the religious connection:

> I suppose it's the same kind of thing people get out of religion... they obviously get something from God to help them through their lives. And Barry is... the same sort of thing. He helps me through my life.[22]

An alternative approach is to internalize the attributes of the star and use these as a guide to action, rather in the way that, according to Julian Jaynes, people in ancient civilizations used the hallucinated voices of their gods for guidance.[23] The following quote is from a fan (retrospectively, as an adult) of the teenage Hollywood film star Deanna Durbin:

> I adored her and my adoration influenced my life a great deal. I wanted to be as much like her as possible, both in my manners and clothes... If I found myself in any annoying or aggravating situation, which I previously dealt with by an outburst of temper, I found myself wondering what Deanna would do and modified my own reactions accordingly.[24]

Another way in which the behaviour of celebrity fans mimics that of religious devotees is in the collection of relics and experiences which are necessary as a rubber-stamp of authenticity: my idol *exists*. For sporting heroes and pop stars, the best way of acquiring this proof is to attend a sporting event or concert in which they are present. As a David Bowie fan in the Vermorels' book suggests:

The clamour for tickets for the '83 concerts was so immense because you are sharing two hours of your life with him – two hours in the life of someone you know won't be there one day. It's quite a marvellous experience to be able to at least say: 'I shared two hours with him.'[25]

However, breathing the same air for two hours may not be enough for more devout followers. They require concrete, tangible proof of mortality which can be jealously possessed. In much the same way that the veneration of saints and martyrs in the fourth century inspired a busy trade in holy relics, so modern-day celebrities have spawned a minor industry whereby value is attached to any item of clothing or other possession that has come into contact with a star, especially if there is some carnal association. For instance, Tudor[26] reports that, among the fan mail for two early Hollywood film stars were requests for 'soap, lipstick tissues, a chewed piece of gum, piece of (your) horse's tail or a lock of your hair, cigarette butt' and even a mere 'blade of grass from the star's lawn'. Other fans have been less restrained; the tearing of pop stars' clothing had become a media cliché by the 1970s, and it is customary for tennis players at tournaments to hurl their own relics (sweat bands and so on) into the audience after a match, where they are savagely fought over. Celebrity autographs are still treasured possessions, though it is better still to be able to *touch* your hero and not wash that part of your body for as long as hygienically possible (and sometimes longer).

Obsessive fans will go further still: there is a classic tale of a Kate Bush fan who rented an apartment in the same block so that he could siphon off her (used) bath water and sell it, bottled, for a tidy sum. The true story of the origins of the bathwater are probably apocryphal, but as with William Ireland's literary relics (see Chapter 2), the truth never stopped the public from parting with their money.

Meet the fans!

In Thomas Hardy's *Jude the Obscure* there is a poignant scene where the hero, Jude Fawley, sets out to meet the composer of his favourite hymn. 'What a man of sympathies he must be!'

muses Jude. 'If there were any one person in the world to choose as a confidant, this composer would be the one, for he must have suffered, and throbbed, and yearned.'[27] Alas, the composer turns out to be more interested in setting up in the wine trade than in unprofitable hymn-writing, and leaves Jude with an impression of 'one of the most commonplace men I ever met'.

What happens when we finally come face-to-face with our idols? For 'Trekkies' this is not a problem: their idols are entirely fictitious, and the pleasure of their fandom lies in their manipulation of media product rather than in the celebration of the actors as 'real' personalities (although not all *Star Trek* fans have the same level of detachment, as will be seen later in the chapter!).

I recently carried out a small survey of Open University students in which I asked them if they had ever come into contact with famous people, and to elaborate if possible. What I was particularly interested in finding out was how, if at all, the encounter changed the respondent's perspective of the star involved. The responses fell largely into three categories:

Enhancement. The first group of encounters were largely positive experiences, where meeting a star, and talking to them, made members of the public more appreciative of the celebrities involved. This was particularly true of category one celebrities, 'public figures' who have gained recognition through their status. One respondent met the general secretary of a leading British trade union at a nursing function; talking to him 'increased my belief in the sincerity of his opinions' and 'increased faith in him as the leader of the Union'. Another respondent recalled meeting a British government adviser and well-known peer who left an 'unforgettable impression' as a public figure who was not only exceptionally perceptive and intelligent, but seemingly unaware of his 'incredible talents'. It is most likely that our impressions of famous people will be enhanced if we are in doubts as to their 'authenticity' or if they reveal an unexpected side to their character which is not evident through their media presentation.

Normalization. The second group of encounters involved a wide range of celebrities whose appearance 'in the flesh' had the effect of normalizing them and removing the mystique surrounding their appearance (this may be the same effect as the frequent comment people make about how much 'smaller' celebrities seem in reality than on television). These encounters can be ones in which a major celebrity has been exposed as a rather minor, even slightly sorry, figure. One respondent recalled meeting a British comic actor at a book signing – to which nobody had turned up and, what's more, on a cold day, 'they made the poor bloke sit by the open doors!' Another met an international footballer as a fellow parent, making him seem 'less intimidating and human'. Even as lofty a figure as Prince Charles was cut down to size when one respondent, the member of a parachute regiment, was introduced to him on a royal visit: 'I felt less in awe as meeting him made him real...He looked just like anyone else who is short and bald.' Generally speaking, the effect of normalization should be more extreme the more remote the celebrity seems.

Disillusionment. The final group of encounters reflected those of Jude Fawley, where the celebrated person turns out to be a disappointment, or worse. For several months, the British 'adult comic' *Viz* carried a feature (whose title I shan't repeat here) which invited readers to send in examples of celebrities who had brazenly abused fans and other members of the public; they were inundated with responses. In my survey, one or two respondents mentioned being introduced to celebrities at parties and being cold-shouldered (the celebrity not even bothering to make small talk). One woman recalls meeting a presenter of the BBC children's show *Blue Peter* 'hiding under the stairs' at St Paul's Cathedral, where he was apparently taking refuge from a group of schoolchildren who had spotted him! Alas, he turned out to be, on acquaintance, 'a bit of a slimeball'. But the worst example came from an apprentice builder who had worked on the house of a former Scottish footballer turned television pundit:

> Before, he seemed quite plausible and easy-going, but after working on his house, and my personal experience of him as a real person, my attitude changed dramatically...even on saying good morning to him I was completely ignored, and this got worse on a daily basis ...later he mentioned to my boss that he hated workmen in his house!

As discussed in the previous chapter, one of the great pressures of celebrity life is the need to maintain a consistent presentation of self in every public context. Letting your mask slip can be a costly business.

For some members of the public, their encounters with stars not only turn out to be enhancing experiences, but blossom into full-blown relationships. Not every anonymous member of the public is a nuisance. For example, pop stars Gary Numan and Adam Ant are both reported to be living with former female fans. As a note of encouragement to stalkers everywhere, the American actor Luke Perry is said to be married to a woman who first attracted his attention by sending him an item of underwear through the post.[28] And, as I have mentioned before, the difference between a fan and a celebrity is often only a matter of time. TV presenter Anthea Turner is said to have been a teenage fan of Peter Powell during his days as a Radio 1 disc jockey. When she became a celebrity in her own right she not only got to meet her former idol but ended up marrying him.

Stars in danger

> Patrick Stewart, the British actor who plays Captain Jean-Luc Picard in *Star Trek*, has hired bodyguards to protect him from a psychopathic stalker who has been following him around the world for over two years. The Shakespearean actor has resorted to such extreme measures, which also include employing private detectives to put the stalker under 24-hour surveillance, to defend himself and his fiancée.[29]

Stewart's tale is all too commonplace in Hollywood (where celebrities are relatively easy to trace) as well as in other parts of the world. For people who have already begun to tire of the public recognition and the letters from suicidal fans, stalkers are one more hazard for celebrities to deal with.

What does 'stalking' involve? According to a study cited in the above *Observer* report, it is behaviour which troubles well over a million men and women each year in the United States. Double that and you have a very large number of people throughout the world who are stalking or being stalked, which suggests that the criteria for definition are rather loose.

This might make it hard for a celebrity to distinguish between over-enthusiastic fans and genuinely dangerous individuals. Clearly it is not possible for a top star to be 'stalked' by several hundred autograph-book-wielding fans simultaneously, so a genuine stalker would be the fan who is making an extra special effort, either through travel or through some other means of devotion.

Even so, the difference between a devotee and a stalker might be that the latter carries an implied threat of violence (or at least of extremely unpredictable and/or disturbing behaviour). Otherwise we would have to label Jona MacDonald as a stalker. She is cited by Sheryl Garratt as an obsessive fan of Chris Hughes, former drummer with Adam and the Ants.[30] Even after Hughes was no longer a member of the band, she sat on the steps of the Abbey Road studios in London for 110 days and nights while he produced another band's LP. Truly obsessive behaviour, yet hardly meriting a bodyguard.

Is the 'stalker' a typical fan whose devotion has pushed him or her to pathological extremes? Or is it an extraordinary pattern of behaviour, symptomatic of some other unrelated psycho-pathological condition? The research findings are inconclusive. A number of forensic psychologists examined the contents of a large sample of 'inappropriate' letters to celebrities and found that there were a number of factors which predicted whether or not the sender had attempted to make face-to-face contact with the celebrity.[31] Not surprisingly, the most successful predictors were statements in the letters which related to specific times and dates of proposed encounters, and attempts by the sender to obscure his or her whereabouts. However, the presence of threats to harm the celebrity was not a good predictor, nor was the presence of 'enclosures' – objects other than the letter. These provided a fascinating psychological study by themselves, ranging from the innocuous (business cards, media clippings), to the gruesome (a syringe of blood, animal faeces, and even the severed head of a coyote), to the eccentric (a toy submarine, a half-eaten 'candy' bar and a disposable razor).[32]

One reason why we might expect fans to try and contact celebrities is that they are sexually attracted to the celebrity. However this was not found by the above researchers to predict approach. A study by Laura Leets and colleagues found that, among university students who expressed interest in contacting celebrities, sexual attraction was more likely to result in fantasy creation rather than actual attempts to make sexual contact.[33] The authors suggest that maybe the difference between ordinary fans and stalkers is that the latter type of fan is unable to counter their (inappropriate) fantasies with a 'realistic assessment'.

Nevertheless, identifying potential 'stalkers' is an important task for forensic researchers, since the stakes are very high. In 1990 California became the first state to adopt an anti-stalking statute when Rebecca Schaeffer, the star of the sitcom *My Sister Sam*, answered the door of her home to an obsessive fan who, when she refused him entry, broke in and shot her dead. The fatal shooting of John Lennon by a psychopathic fan, Mark Chapman, is now an indelible part of popular music history.

The most celebrated stalker of all time is probably John Hinckley Jr., the man who shot and wounded former US president Ronald Reagan in 1980. Hinckley was not an obsessive fan of Reagan, however, but of the actress Jodie Foster, who was highly traceable as a student at Yale. There seems little doubt that Hinckley was as committed to seeking his own fame as to his passion for Foster, having initially attempted both musical and acting careers. Eventually though he became fixated on a celebrity and bombarded her with letters and poems and other protestations of love, slipping them under her dormitory door. It was a highly successful strategy, as made clear in a letter to Foster:

> I feel very good about the fact that you at least know my name and how I feel about you. And by hanging around your dormitory I've come to realize that I'm the topic of more than a little conversation, however full of ridicule it may be. At least you'll know that I'll always love you.[34]

Eventually, after being continually ignored by the star, Hinckley resorted to extreme measures. He was later found not guilty by a court, by reason of insanity.

How would Hinckley fit into the typology described in the last chapter? It is hard to say. He would seem an obvious choice for the 'accidental fame' category (category four) except that his attempted assassination of Reagan was carried out in a desperate and, more importantly, *deliberate* attempt to demonstrate his love for Foster. In one sense, along with the Kray twins and potentially numerous other celebrated felons, Hinckley could be regarded as the ultimate category three celebrity, whose guiding principle is that fame, rather than achievement, is the ultimate goal. Hinckley just wanted to be known by the world, so that Foster would have to acknowledge him. The means of achieving that fame were largely immaterial.

What is clear to any celebrity is that it is not just your own personal stalker who puts your life at risk. Günther Parche was an obsessive fan of the tennis player Steffi Graf; he became frustrated at the fact that his heroine kept being beaten by the rising star Monica Seles. At a tournament in Hamburg in 1993, Parche waited until a changeover between games, leaned over the barrier and plunged a nine-inch knife into Seles's back, leaving a physical wound one-and-a-half inches deep and a mental scar which took rather longer to heal. A year after the attack she told reporters that she was haunted by images of Parche's face ('I see the knife every night'). It took her another year before she felt able to return to public competition.[35]

Clearly, no entourage of minders can protect other celebrities from random assault. It is a peril the famous have to live with. Will John Hinckley Jr. ever become the target of a stalker himself? It would complete a rather neat circle.

Conclusion

Some might doubt whether parasocial relationships are really worthy of the term 'relationship'. In this chapter I hope I have demonstrated otherwise: parasocial interaction involves celebrities in a way that can be both rewarding and life-threatening. The sheer number of modern celebrities is such that many adult members of the public have encountered a star in person at least once in their lifetime. These encounters may enhance the reputation of the star, 'normalize' them or even damage previously favourable impressions. And where parasocial relationships with celebrities are sufficiently powerful to warrant the term 'fandom', the chance of the fan meeting the star is quite high. The history of fandom is full of parallels with the history of religion. This is not to devalue, or 'pathologize', the media fan whose devotion is centred around a specific show or genre; however, when the intense interest focuses on a single individual, it has important implications for the celebrity herself. The obsessive fan who camps on the star's doorstep has the potential to become either a murderer or a marriage partner. The difference between the devoted admirer and the dangerous 'stalker' may be alarmingly narrow.

Chapter 9

Postscript: the future of celebrity

In Britain, one of the most potent signifiers of fame is an appearance on the television show *This Is Your Life*. The programme is carefully prepared far in advance; extensive research is conducted in order to unearth a celebrity's old school friends and, where possible, any famous faces who have had professional contact with the show's subject. All this takes place unbeknown to the celebrity, usually via a partner or close relative, and then, in order to film the show in front of a studio audience, the show's presenter appears wherever the star happens to be that evening, and presents a mock photo album to the star with the words: '(Celebrity X), *this is your life!*'

For many years, *This is Your Life* was aimed essentially at stars in their twilight years, entertainers who had trod the boards since the days of traditional music hall, and this provided the production team with a wealth of stars, past and present, whom they could contact and feature on the show. Nostalgia was an important element. Then, as the 1980s progressed, the average age of the show's subjects began to plummet. Frequently it featured stars who were in the first flush of fame, who had very little history, and so the roll-call of participants had to be made up of young, current stars. By 1998 the show was featuring members of the public who had led interesting or worthy lives, such as a Yorkshire street sweeper who had been awarded the MBE.

Are we witnessing an important sea-change in the history of fame? Has mass communication made it so easy to obtain fame that it is not worth bothering any more? It is a distinct possibility; and yet the celebrity PR machine rumbles on and sales of tabloid newspapers – whose life blood is the celebrities and the 'filthy goddess' rumour – continue to hold up. More than ever, celebrities are used to promote television shows, films and – notably – traditional art forms such as serious fiction and 'classical' music.

There are other social factors that may keep the celebrity circus running for a while longer. As the research on parasocial interaction suggests, many people use television as a way of combating loneliness; with a trend towards single living, particularly among young people, the uses and gratifications of parasocial relationships may become increasingly important as society fragments further.

However, given that celebrity is a phenomenon constructed through the media, clues to the future of celebrity are seemingly dependent on technological changes affecting television, and so I shall begin this final chapter with a brief overview of the possibilities for television in the twentieth century.

Technological change?

Neuman suggests two fundamental approaches to mass communication.[1] The first is the 'Orwellian' approach, based on the 'predictions' of George Orwell's novel *1984*, which treats technological advance as inherently hostile, with the prospect of television that you can't switch off, beaming political propaganda into every home, rather in the style that Cantril and Allport envisaged for radio.[2]

Neuman constrasts this approach with that of Orwell's contemporary Vannevar Bush (the godfather, in some respects, of the modern computer), who treats it optimistically, as a liberating force. Bush sees modern technology as essentially under the control of the individual, as a largely benign force that, as a later writer has put it, might enable 'our children's children [to]...become the first genius generation'.[3] Bush saw communication evolving alongside society, rather than as a tool of the administration. Some support for the Bush position comes from the work of Christopher Arterton, who investigated a number of situations where innovative technological tools were used in policy making, and concluded that technological advance rarely seems to pull culture, or behaviour; it is usually the other way round.[4] However, this argument was based on a number of one-off episodes where computers had been drafted in to facilitate a task, and the people performing the task preferred to revert to traditional methods when given a choice.[5]

There seem to be a number of different stances that are currently taken with regard to technological futures. One is the nostalgic stance, where people worry about the devaluation of cultural standards; we can see this in some of the psychological research into the 'damaging effects' of television and even in Braudy's disparagement of the 'fame of the moment'. Few people adopt a truly Orwellian stance today, mainly because the positive effects of television have generally outweighed the negative ones, apart from the inconvenience of the adverts. A second stance is the rampant technophilia of computer buffs, who are so excited by the potential for change enabled by computer technology that they are swept along in flights of fancy about the life-changing potential of multimedia and the Internet; the third stance is that adopted by people such as educationalists and ex-hippies who worry about losing touch, and so endorse computer use wherever and whenever possible, just to appear trendy. 'It's going to happen eventually', they say, 'so why fight it?' A fourth, related, stance, is that of marginal groups and radicals who see the Internet as an unpoliced environment for free exchange of subversive ideas, and 'cyberspace' as a liberating site for further fragmentation of the nasty, capitalist, individuated self.

In the United States, the proportion of prime-time viewing shared by the major TV channels has dropped from 90 per cent in the 1970s to 65 per cent by 1990.[6] This fall has been attributed to the proliferation of independent channels; a similar picture may also be true in Britain (albeit to a lesser extent). The deregulation, and digitization, of television are the first of many challenges the medium faces in the twenty-first century. A good summary of the overall situation can be found in a paper by Steemers, who suggests that much of the hype surrounding digital choice is somewhat transparent; the real changes that we see are the result of deregulation.[7] She also suggests that many media servies, such as 'video-on-demand' and even 'pay-per-view', do not really constitute broadcasting as such, and could be described as 'point-to-point communication', which takes them out of the control of those bodies which have traditionally administered broadcast services.

One possibility is that the future may belong to 'narrowcast media' – special interest communications. This can already be seen in Internet technology, where users have complete control over access to information, and would constitute a major step away from the kind of 'national identity' forged since the early days of radio.[8] This of course may make it harder in the long run for as many individuals to gain celebrity status, since much of the modern-day celebrity circus exists around a common cultural link between television and the tabloid press – a link which would be severed if the concept of national television were dissolved. The explosion of channels brought about by deregulation has already made public access television less rewarding to appear on: if none of your friends or colleagues has seen the show (there being only a small probability that they will be watching that particular channel at that particular time), your appearance will provoke little interest. The more people who take part in public access television, the less remarkable will each appearance be. 'Oh, you were on Oprah, were you? I'm going to be on Jerry Springer next week, and my next-door neighbour is on Leeza the week after.'

On the positive side, many people welcome the idea of a 'global village', particularly certain ethnic minority groups, who have already been active in the creation of 'cybercommunities' (or 'diasporic web sites'), via the Internet, which transcend geographical boundaries.[9] One aspect of technology which has considerable implications for the future of celebrity is virtual reality (VR). At present, VR is little more than a toy for boffins, or a research tool, but in years to come it may find itself incorporated into mass communications.

Some media commentators, such as Shapiro and McDonald, argue that VR, if allied to mass media, 'is as likely to shape our attitudes, beliefs and behaviors as other forms of mass media'.[10] Their argument is that VR-enhanced special effects will simply intensify the experience of watching television – making the impact of, say, a car crash or a shooting on screen twice as realistic. At present, the virtual environment can only be experienced through the use of special headsets, and while users have to rely on cumbersome apparatus, VR is unlikely to have much impact. However, incorporating it into conventional media forms is a possibility and, as Shapiro and McDonald suggest, it may in future produce 'media forms we can't imagine now'.[11] A particularly exciting development in prospect is that of 'holography', a form of technology which can make people and places appear and move as though actually in the room in which the viewer is watching. This is likely to have an even greater impact than VR, although it may not be developed until well into the twenty-first century.[12] The implications of holographic television for parasocial interaction are particularly interesting.

Champions of Internet technology may well argue that television is an antiquated technological form, that already people are abandoning their sets in favour of the enriching possibilities of cyberspace. One particularly vocal proponent of cybertechnology is Sherry Turkle, who takes a firm postmodernist line on the evolution of the self.[13] For her, the Net has transformed the presentation of self because it acts as a *tabula rasa* for identity: you can 'be' who you like as you interact in a virtual environment. Turkle focuses her research on what are known as multi-user domains (MUDs), which are user ('chat') groups and role-playing environments in which 'virtual personae' interact with one another, for example by creating mini-programs and inviting other users to respond. Turkle's participants are not casual users; one woman claims to spend up to five hours a day in MUDs, while others become highly emotionally involved (there have been serious charges made of 'virtual rape'). Turkle is keen to stress the active nature of cyberlife – like Harry Jenkins's media fans (discussed in Chapter 8), the contents of cyberspace are there to be reinterpreted so that the user becomes the creator, unlike the passive consumer of television.[14]

It is hard, though, to imagine that cyberspace will exert the same pull for the majority of the population as it does for Turkle's highly unusual participants. Much of her evidence for the decentring of self rests on what are really little more than *games*, and the liberating qualities of cyberspace, while fun in the short term, may become frustrating. Turkle talks of 'TinySex' (e-mail erotica), but some recent research suggests that even the heaviest users of e-mail groups are using the net as little more than a glorified dating agency – many e-mail users go on to meet electronically acquired acquaintances in real life, and several have even become romantically involved as a direct consequence.[15] Much of the time, like pornography, TinySex may be no more than a substitute for real sexual interaction, at best a prelude to the act itself.

Winston[16] is highly sceptical about some of the claims made for cyberspace, particularly the use of the term 'information revolution'. Real change is, he argues, essentially a *slow* process (and computer buffs often forget how, even at the end of the twentieth century, only a tiny proportion of the world's population has access to the net – you have to buy a computer first, and they don't come cheap). Radical claims made on behalf of the liberating nature of the net are absurdly optimistic, he argues; already there is increasing pressure to suppress the use of the net for distributing pornography, and increasing policing will eventually turn the information highway into a toll road. Virtual communities are no more revolutionary than any other 'hobby'. Most significantly, he argues that 'one of the sillier facets of the revolutionary rhetoric' of computer buffs is the idea that the Internet will free us from the apparently intolerable burdens of shopping and travel. Nonsense, Winston argues; since mass communication opened the world up there has been more shopping and travel than ever before, and 'the only effective marketers in the... information highway [have been] pornographers.'[17]

As I see it, there are three possible outcomes for television in the twenty-first century:

1. *Emergence of media hierarchies.* The extraordinary success of (early) television in meeting, and creating, human needs suggests that it might serve as a model for future development. There is already talk of a 'golden age' of television, and where in the 1970s there was a strong backlash against 'repeats' of old television programmes, the modern trend is for satellite channels such as UK Gold and Granada Plus to be created solely as outlets for endless 'repeats'. One possibility is that television has progressed so rapidly that it has already passed through all possible cycles and creatively bankrupted itself. The other possibility is that, as the number of channels multiplies, as with the Internet, users have too much control over access, and television is no longer a valuable medium for communication.

One way of dealing with this is for certain channels to become prioritized so that, rather than just 'being on television', one has to appear on such-and-such a channel to be truly worthy of respect. Eventually it may be that TV channels become more like newspapers, geared towards specific audiences, with interactive multimedia features built in. The advent of teletext, already used as a daily newspaper substitute by many, has been a major step in this direction.

2. *The death of television.* If the Internet takes over our lives, as computer buffs hope it will, then what use is television? What use is *anything*, if it can be summoned through the net like a genie from a magic lamp? Books will disappear from our shelves, CDs – like LPs before them – will cower in the corner of the room. We will need no more information than that which we receive at will from our computer. Television will simply become one of a multitude of computer functions; already we can call up practically any film we wish to see (so videos, and video rental companies, will pack up), and TV programmes will be submerged beneath several tons of information rubble, to be sought out and downloaded by the afficionado. Face it: most of what we watch is trash; why watch trash when you can have gold at the touch of a button? As trash disappears from our screens, we will find better ways to fill our evenings...

We (computer buffs aside) tend to react with horror at the thought of such a prospect. In the last 50 years we have grown so used to our record and CD collections as forming a major part of our identity, and our choice of television programme indicates taste, discernment and character. But these things have, historically speaking, appeared overnight; they may slink back into obscurity equally quickly.

3. *Continuous adaptation.* The final, and most likely, scenario is the least interesting and spectacular. If television has changed our lives so profoundly as I have suggested in this book, then why has so much else survived? While everything around them changed, the traditional arts, particularly theatre and classical music, survived. The Albert Hall in London is filled every summer for the Prom concerts, and the Royal Shakespeare Company still sell out wherever they perform. There have been slight adjustments to keep pace with the times: for instance, the classical music world has embraced modern marketing principles and has opened up to less traditional forms, while still

retaining many of its traditional structures. Theatre, likewise, has developed so fast that it is hard to shock even mainstream audiences any more. Maybe television too will retain its audience simply through its already rich heritage, however hard it is kicked by the jackboots of the cyberpolice.

Fame and celebrity are unlikely to perish just because television loses its pride of place in our lives. Sport, for example, will continue to produce superstars, as will the arts and politics. Since news bulletins and other information outlets prioritize individuals in their stories, there will continue to be people who are famous by accident or by outrageous design. However it is unlikely that they will occupy centre stage in quite the same way as they do now. Television is so important in perpetuating the cult of the celebrity that any changes in its development will be reflected in the number of celebrities that emerge and the reasons for their fame. It may be that the celebrity explosion of recent years is just a blip on the course of cultural history; in 50 years' time it will seem incredible that Paul Nolan or Maureen Reece were ever famous. Fame may revert to what people like Leo Braudy see as its rightful heritage, becoming the preserve of *achievers* – the category two types. As time speeds up further, it will become even harder to predict what will endure; we may stop trying, and put instant fame on hold.

Alternatively, the cult of celebrity may keep growing and growing. Fuelled by the Internet reaching our homes via digital transmission, our needs for parasocial interaction may increase as we spend more time at home (already, 'teleworking' is being used as a money-saving device by businesses), and the media expansion may simply open up more slots of opportunity for new celebrities. After all, that is the way we are heading right now. The shaman's conjuring tent may yet become bigger and better than ever before.

Appendix

Possibilities for future research

If the psychology of fame and celebrity is to become a flourishing research area, it is worth considering some potential avenues for future projects. This book has posed more questions than it attempts to answer – no bad thing, perhaps, when the research topic is in its infancy. Below are a handful of suggested projects.

1. Developing the concept of parasocial relationships

From the perspective of mainstream psychology, this seems like the clearest gap in the current research literature. It would be nice if some experts in the area of human relationships were to contribute to this question – even if they don't like the concept as it stands, they might suggest more appropriate ways of talking about, and researching, parasocial interaction.

2. Developing the taxonomy

The taxonomy I have outlined in Chapter 7 is by no means intended as a definitive model for studying fame. It is a research embryo, awaiting nourishment from other sources. It has to be said that some of the components of the taxonomy may be difficult to research, for instance establishing a clear boundary between national and international fame. If people are intent on quantifying the levels in the taxonomy there may need to be much tedious accumulation of data ahead.

There is also some work to be done on the fourth dimension of the taxonomy – the importance of different types of information about famous people. It would be interesting, for example, to see if there were certain types of celebrity about whom more information could be supplied than for others, and if there were some individuals who were only recognized by a single piece of information (a face or a name). There is a slight problem in using specific faces as stimuli, in that it is hard to achieve experimental control (unless one had access to celebrities to assemble a special set of controlled photographs, which is unlikely). However, there is a large psychological literature on face recognition that could be drawn upon to guide any research on this aspect of the taxonomy.[1]

3. Developing counselling procedures for celebrities

As suggested in Chapter 6, one of the difficulties celebrities face is that so few of them are ready for fame. Very often they have focused only on the positives – the money, the adoration, the plaudits. Celebrities may need psychologists to help them through the first year or two of fame, particularly to deal with the public, and to deal with press attention, especially when it is negative (bad reviews) or intrusive (paparazzi nuisance). Some of the richer stars, especially in Hollywood, already employ mental health professionals, often for exorbitant fees; one of the values of having a thorough academic approach to the psychology of fame is that it gives a sound research base that can inform practice in this area.

4. Exploring fame from other perspectives

Many readers will be unhappy with the way I have dealt with important issues in this book, or by what I have neglected. I am all too aware, for instance, of the great significance that *gender* might have on the impact of, and desire for, fame. There is also much potential in exploring some of the aspects of 'over-involvement' at the level of the viewer or fan which have been pathologized by (male) researchers in the past.

Culture and ethnicity are two other areas which I have neglected. This is a serious omission, given the historically and culturally situated nature of the self, and the important implications this must have for the experience of fame. It might be, for example, that fame is easier to cope with in collectivist cultures where issues such as 'authenticity' are not a problem. Indeed it may be that in such cultures the desire for fame (never mind the mechanisms for producing it) is much less powerful than in the individualist West. Interestingly, there seems to be no overt influence of ethnicity *within* Western culture with regard to the desire for, and experiences of, fame. Perhaps the central aspects of self across cultures are not as different as some researchers may have liked to make out. I would be very interested in any research on fame in other, non-Western cultures, particularly regarding, say, the film stars of 'Bollywood' (Indian cinema).

5. *More reliable interview data from celebrities*

This falls very much into the 'nice work if you can get it' category of research and relies very much on psychologists' powers of negotiation with 'gatekeepers'. (Who might these be in relation to celebrities? Publicists, in my experience, would not be interested in research unless it was to be published in a consumer publication.) However, it is crucial that we gain access to celebrities in order to obtain first-hand accounts of their experiences of fame, and particularly where they might feel they would benefit from the application of psychology.

And finally...

It may of course be that you, the reader, are a celebrity yourself, your curiosity sparked by the word 'psychology' in the book's title. It may be that you have strident objections to many of the assumptions I have been making, or that you would like to follow up some of the points in the book. In either case I would love to hear from you. Research participation is warmly invited.

Notes and References

1 Introduction: defining fame and celebrity

1. Braudy, L. (1997) *The Frenzy of Renown: Fame and its History* (2nd edition). New York: Vintage Books.
2. For the best writing on celebrity from a sociological/cultural studies perspective, see: Gamson, J. (1994) *Claims to Fame: Celebrity in Contemporary America*. Berkeley California. University of California Press; and Marshall, P. D. (1997) *Celebrity and Power: Fame in Contemporary Culture*. Minneapolis: University of Minnesota Press.
3. Marshall, ibid.
4. Boorstin, D. J. (1961) *The Image: A Guide to Pseudo-events in America*. New York: Harper & Row, p. 57.
5. Braudy, *The Frenzy of Renown*.
6. Moran, J. (1998) 'Cultural studies and academic stardom'. *International Journal of Cultural Studies*, 1, pp. 67–82 an interesting paper which tackles the issue of 'academic celebrity'. Moran argues that, owing (partly) to the pressures exerted by the Research Assessment Exercise in British universities, a star system has developed, which conflicts with the egalitarian ethos of disciplines such as cultural studies.
7. Sean French, 'Diary'. *New Statesman*, 16 June 1989.

2 'Mad for noblesse': fame through history

1. Jaynes, J. (1976, 1990) *The Origin of Consciousness in the Breakdown of the Bicameral Mind*. London: Penguin.
2. Braudy, L. (1986, 1997) *The Frenzy of Renown: Fame and its History*. New York: Vintage Books. All page references relating to this text are from the later edition.
3. Ibid., p. 32.
4. Ibid., p. 57.
5. Ibid., p. 104.
6. Ibid., p. 152.
7. Ibid., p. 232.

8. Dante Alighieri (1955) *The comedy of Dante Alighieri, the Florentine: Cartica 2: Purgatory (IL Purgatorio,* trans. D. L. Sayers. London: Penguin.
9. Chaucer, G. (1957) *The Works of Geoffrey Chaucer* (2nd Edition). London University Press.
10. Braudy, *The Frenzy of Renown*, p. 306.
11. Ibid., p. 266.
12. Ibid., p. 267.
13. Ibid., p. 393.
14. Ibid., p. 372.
15. Ibid., p. 373.
16. Ibid., p. 425.
17. Gamson, J. (1994) *Claims to Fame: Celebrity in Contemporary America.* Berkeley, California, University of California Press; Marshall, P. D. (1997) *Celebrity and Power: Fame in Contemporary Culture.* Minneapolis: University of Minnesota Press.
18. Marshall, *Celebrity and Power*, p. xi.
19. An important reference here is R. G. Thomson (ed.) (1996) *Freakery: Cultural Spectacles of the Extraordinary Body.* New York University Press. B. Lindfors' Chapter, 'Ethological show business: Footlighting the dark continent', describes the unbelievably cruel and dehumanizing display of Africans in Europe during the nineteenth century.
20. Gamson, *Claims to Fame*, p. 21.
21. Gerber, D. A. (1996) 'The "careers" of people exhibited, In R. G. Thomson (ed.) *Freakery: Cultural Spectacles of the Extraordinary body.* New York University Press, pp. 38–54.
22. Cook, J. W. Jr. (1996) 'Of men, missing links, and nondescripts: The strange career of P.T. Barnum's "What is It?" exhibition'. In R. G.Thomson (ed.) *Freakery:* pp. 139–57.
23. Marshall, *Celebrity and Power.*
24. Staiger, J. (1991) 'Seeing stars'. In C. Gledhill (ed.) *Stardom: Industry of Desire.* London: Routledge, pp. 3–16.
25. Cited in Gamson, *Claims to Fame*, p. 35.
26. Gamson, ibid., p. 29.
27. Gledhill, C. (1991) 'Introduction'. In C. Gledhill (ed.) *Stardom: Industry of Desire.* London: Routledge, pp. xiii–xx.
28. *Daily Telegraph*, 23 August 1996.
29. Scannell, P. and Cardiff, D. (1991) *A Social History of British Broadcasting.* Oxford: Blackwell.
30. Walker, A. (1970) *Stardom: The Hollywood Phenomenon.* New York: Stein and Day.
31. Buxton, D. (1990) 'Rock music, the star system, and the rise of consumerism'. In S. Frith and A. Goodwin (eds) *On Record: Rock, Pop and the Written Word.* London: Routledge, pp. 427–40.

32. Winstone, R. (ed.) (1996) *The Benn Diaries*. London: Arrow.
33. Healey, D. (1989) *The Time of my Life*. London: Penguin.
34. Marshall, *Celebrity and Power*, is a valuable reference for discussion of the media construction of political leaders.
35. Pearson, J. (1995) *The Profession of Violence: The Rise and Fall of the Kray Twins* (4th edition). London: HarperCollins, p. 41.
36. Ibid., p. 85.
37. Reported in *The Times*, 1 September 1998.
38. See Gledhill, *Stardom*.
39. Yuan, D. D. (1996) 'The celebrity freak: Michael Jackson's "Grotesque Glory"'. In R. G.Thomson (ed.) *Freakery: Cultural Spectacles of the Extraordinary Body*. New York University Press, pp. 368–84.
40. Taraborelli, J. R. (1992) *Michael Jackson: The Magic and the Madness*. New York: Ballantine, p. 388.
41. Jackson claims otherwise; he is seeking to become the 'universal man' (see Yuan, 'The Celebrity Freak', for full details of the Jackson saga).

3 The quest for fame

1. Rogan, J. (1992) *Morrissey and Marr: The Severed Alliance*. London: Omnibus, p. 92.
2. Reynolds, S. (1990) *Blissed out: The Raptures of Rock*. London: Serpent's Tail, p. 25.
3. Ibid, p. 25.
4. Simonton, D. K. (1994) *Greatness: Who Makes History and Why*. New York: Guilford Press.
5. Pearson, J. (1995) *The Profession of Violence: The Rise and Fall of the Kray Twins* (4th edition). London: HarperCollins.
6. Claims to have identified the genetic basis of homosexuality have generated more media publicity than the research findings have perhaps warranted. Nevertheless, one leading US biologist (Simon LeVay) has been quoted in *Newsweek* (24 February 1992) as saying that he would 'give up a scientific career altogether' if unsuccessful in his attempt to demonstrate inherited differences in neurological structure between homosexual and heterosexual men (so much for scientific research starting out from the position of the null hypothesis!).
7. The Krays, of course, are a 'single case' from which it would be unfair to generalise; for a thorough tarring- and-feathering of identical twin research, see Rose, S., Lewontin, R. C. and Kamin, L. J. (1984) *Not in our Genes: Biology, Ideology and Human Nature*. London: Penguin.
8. Simonton, *Greatness*, p. 35.

NOTES AND REFERENCES   161

9. Gedo, J. E. (1996) *The Artist and the Emotional World*. New York: Columbia University Press.
10. Milton, J. (1989) *Paradise Lost*, trans. C. Ricks, London: Penguin.
11. Jaynes, J. (1976) *The Origin of consciousness in the Breakdown of the Bicameral Mind*. London: Penguin.
12. Simonton, *Greatness*.
13. Braudy, L. (1997) *The Frenzy of Renown: Fame and its History* (2nd edition). New York: Vintage Books, p. 84.
14. Cited in Clark, R. W. (1980) *Freud*. New York: Random House, p. 19.
15. Adler, A. (1938) *Social Interest* (J. Linton and R. Vaughan, trans.). London: Faber & Faber.
16. Campbell, D. T. (1960) 'Blind variation and selective retention in creative thought as in other knowledge processes'. *Psychological Review*, 67, pp. 380–400 (quoted in Simonton, *Greatness*., p. 166).
17. Simonton, *Greatness*., p. 170.
18. However, it should be noted that during 1998 a number of British government ministers were 'outed' as homosexual.
19. Cicero, M. T. (45 BC, 1943). 'Tusculan disputations'. In J. E. King (trans.) *Cicero in twenty-eight volumes, No. 18*. London: William Heinemann.
20. Jamison, K. R. (1989) 'Mood disorders and patterns of creativity in British writers and artists'. *Psychiatry*, 52, pp. 125–34.
21. Gedo, *The Artist and the Emotional World*, pp. 96–97.
22. Erikson, E. H. (1950) *Childhood and Society*. New York: Norton.
23. McAdams, D. P. and de St. Aubin, E. (1992) 'A theory of generativity and its assessment through self-report, behavioral acts, and narrative themes in autobiography'. *Journal of Personality and Social Psychology*, 62, pp. 1003–15.
24. See McAdams, D. P. (1985) *Power, Intimacy and the Life Story: Persological Inquiries into Identity*. New York: Guilford Press.
25. Kotre, J. (1996) *Outliving the Self: How We Live on in Future Generations*. New York: Norton.
26. Braudy, *The Frenzy of Renown*, p. 223.
27. The best writing on this topic can be found in Parker, I. (1992) *Discourse Dynamics: Critical Analysis for Social and Individual Psychology*. London: Routledge; and Edwards, D. (1996) *Discourse and Cognition*. London: Sage.
28. Braudy, *The Fenzy of Renown*, p. 55.
29. Sandeen, C. (1997) 'Success defined by television: The value system promoted by *PM* magazine'. *Critical Studies in Mass Communication*, 14, pp. 77–105.
30. Marshall, P. D. (1997) *Celebrity and Power: Fame in Contemporary Cultur*. Minneepotis: University of Minnesota Press.
31. Gamson, J. (1994) *Claims to Fame Celebrity in Contemporary America*, Berkeley, CA: University of California Press, p. 88.

32. 'Evolutionary psychology' has become a popular branch of the discipline, inspired by advances in genetics. Nobody has written about genetics better, or more influentially, than the zoologist Richard Dawkins (*The Selfish Gene*, Oxford University Press 1976/ 1989). Dawkins is ambivalent about the influence of 'genes' on human behaviour – indeed, he claims that 'we, alone on earth, are able to rebel against the tyranny of the selfish replicator' (ibid., p. 202). Others are less guarded, notably the biologist Robin Baker, whose *Sperm Wars* (1996) is, I think, a spectacularly misguided effort to apply the principles of animal behaviour to human sexual activity.
33. *Western Daily News*, 24 December 1997.
34. Dawkins, *The Selfish Gene*. Dawkins coined the term 'selfish gene' to counter arguments by earlier biologists that the 'unit' of natural selection might be family relatedness or even the species as a whole. Ultimately, Dawkins argues, all acts of apparent self-sacrifice can be interpreted as beneficial to the individual – therefore it would seem more likely that, rather than perpetuating a family line, reproduction is primarily geared to replicating one's own DNA as faithfully as possible. An objection to the term *selfish* might be that the attribution of selfishness to bits of DNA is at best anthropomorphic; at worst, liable to create unwarranted, and potentially dangerous, assumptions about animal (and human) behaviour.
35. I have attempted, wherever possible, to avoid using the term 'homosexuals' to denote a class of individuals. Michel Foucault argued (*The History of Sexuality*, Vol. 1, Penguin, 1981) that the term 'homosexual' used, prior to the Victorian era, to refer to a sexual practice rather than a class of person ('The sodomite had been a temporary aberration; the homosexual was now a species'). This is not linguistic pedantry; sexuality is, of course, a complex and elusive matter! If I refer to 'homosexuals' or 'homosexual individuals', then, I am referring to people whose dominant and preferred mode of sexual congress is with individuals of the same gender.
35. Braudy, *The Frenzy of Renown*.
37. Braudy, ibid.
38. Both this, and the earlier Daguerre comment, quoted in Tagg, J. (1988) *The Burden of Representation: Essays on Photographies and Histories*. Basingstoke: Macmillan, p. 41.
39. Harvey, D. (1990) *The Condition of Postmodernity*. Cambridge, MA: Blackwell, p. 289.
40. A form of interaction which has been called 'parasocial interaction', and will be discussed at length in the next chapter.

4 Fame and the 'general public'

1. The use of the word 'effects' in relation to the psychological processing of media is a matter of some dispute. Often 'effects' is used uncritically, without any causal relationship having been established between stimulus and response. Here I would like to draw the reader's attention to Barker and Petley's *Ill Effects: The Media/Violence Debate* (Routledge, 1997), especially Ian Vine's chapter, 'The dangerous psycho-logic of media effects'.
2. Cantril, H. and Allport, G. (1935) *The Psychology of Radio*. New York: Harper & Brothers.
3. Himmelweit, H. T., Oppenheim, A. N. and Vince, P. (1958) *Television and the child*. London: Oxford University Press. A typical example of early 'television and psychology' texts.
4. Barker & Petley, *Ill Effects*. This edited book is a critical examination of the 'video nasty' moral panic, and is particularly scathing towards some of the claims made by child psychologists following the James Bulger murder trial in the early 1990s. Other work on children and television has been conducted by Barrie Gunter and colleagues: Gunter, B. and McAleer, J. (1997) *Children and television* (Routledge) is a comprehensive overview of most of the important issues.
5. Gunter, B. (1987) *Poor Reception: Misunderstanding and Forgetting Broadcast News*. Hillsdale, NJ: Lawrence Erlbaum Associates.
6. Newhagen, J. E. and Reeves, B. (1992) 'The evening's bad news: Effects of compelling negative television news imagery'. *Journal of Communication*, 42, pp. 25–41.
7. Comstock, G., Chaffee, S., Katzman, N., McCombs, M. and Roberts, D. (1978) *Television and Human Behavior*. New York: Columbia University Press.
8. Harris, R. J. (1991) *The Cognitive Psychology of Mass Communication*. Hillsdale, NJ: Lawrence Erlbaum Associates.
9. Condry, J. (1989) *The Psychology of Television*. Hillsdale, NJ: Lawrence Erlbaum Associates.
10. Kubey, R. and Csikszentmihalyi, M. (1990) *Television and the Quality of Life: How Viewing Shapes Everyday Experience*. Hillsdale, NJ: Lawrence Erlbaum Associates.
11. Ibid., p. 201.
12. A more positive, and less snobbish, up-to-date critique of television culture can be found in Ellis Cashmore's *... And then there was television* (Routledge, 1994).
13. More recently, Tony Charlton has been investigating the introduction of television to the Atlantic island of St Helena and found a number of changes in schoolchildren's behaviour. For a reference, try: Charlton, T., Coles, D. and Lovemore, T. (1997) Teachers' ratings

of nursery class children's behaviour before and after availability of television by satellite'. *Psychological Reports*, 81, pp. 96–8.
14. Williams, T. M. (1985) 'Implications of a natural experiment in the developed world for research on television in the developing world'. *Journal of Cross Cultural Psychology*, 16, pp. 263–87.
15. Newton, A. J. and Buck, E. B. (1985) 'Television as significant other: Its relationship to self-descriptors in five developing countries'. *Journal of Cross Cultural Psychology*, 16, pp. 289–312.
16. Noble, G. (1975) *Children in front of the small screen*. Beverly Hills, CA: Sage.
17. Granzberg, G. (1985) 'Television and self-concept formation in developing areas: The central Canadian Algonkian experience'. *Journal of Cross Cultural Psychology*, 16, p. 323.
18. Shapiro, M. A. and McDonald, D. G. (1995) 'I'm not a real doctor, but I play one in virtual reality: Implications of virtual reality for judgments about reality'. In F. Biocca and M. R. Levy (eds) *Communication in the Age of Virtual Reality*. Hillsdale, NJ: Lawrence Erlbaum Associates, pp. 323–45.
19. Gunter and McAleer, *Children and Television*.
20. Samuels, A. and Taylor, M. (1994) 'Children's ability to distinguish fantasy events from real-life events'. *British Journal of Developmental Psychology*, 12, pp. 417–27.
21. A useful reference here is Maire Messenger Davies' *Fake, Fact and Fantasy: Children's Interpretations of Television Reality* (Hills dale, NJ: Lawrence Erlbaum Associates, 1997).
22. Reeves, B. and Nass, C. (1996) *The Media Equation: How People Treat Computers, Television, and New Media Like Real People and Places*. Stanford University: Cambridge University Press.
23. Ibid., p. 11.
24. Bianculli, D. (1992) *Tele-literacy: Taking Television Seriously*. New York: Continuum.
25. Hodge, B. and Tripp, D. (1986) *Children and Television*. Cambridge: Polity Press.
26. Rice, M. L., Huston, A. C. and Wright, J. C. (1983) 'The forms of television: Effects on children's attention, comprehension, and social behaviour'. In M. Meyer (ed.) *Children and the Formal Features of Television: Approaches and Findings of Experimental and Formative Research*. Munich: K. G. Saur.
27. Davies, *Fake, Fact and Fantasy*.
28. Stacey, J. (1991) 'Feminine fascinations: Forms of identification in star-audience relations'. In C. Gledhill (ed.) *Stardom: Industry of Desire*. London: Routledge, pp. 141–66.
29. Cohen, J. and Metzger, M. (1998) 'Social affiliation and the achievement of ontological security through interpersonal and mass communication'. *Critical Studies in Mass Communication*, 15, pp. 41–60.

30. Horton, D. and Wohl, R. R. (1956) 'Mass communication and parasocial interaction'. *Psychiatry*, 19, pp. 215–29.
31. Ibid., p. 216
32. Scannell, P. (1996) *Radio, Television and Modern Life*. Oxford: Blackwell, p. 19.
33. Rubin, R. B. & McHugh, M. P. (1987) 'Development of parasocial interaction relationships'. *Journal of Broadcasting and Electronic Media*, 31, pp. 279–92.
34. Harris, *Cognitive Psychology*.
35. Rubin, A. M., Perse, E. M., & Powell, R. A. (1985) 'Loneliness, parasocial interaction, and local television news viewing'. *Human Communication Research*, 12, pp. 155–80.
36. Indeed, as this book goes to press, I am in the process of piloting a parasocial interaction scale targeted specifically at British media users.
37. Cortez, C. A. (1992) 'Mediated interpersonal communication: The role of attraction and perceived homophily in the development of parasocial relationships'. Doctoral dissertation, University of Iowa.
38. Picirillo, M. S. (1986) 'On the authenticity of televisual experience: A critical exploration of parasocial closure'. *Critical Studies in Mass Communication*, 3, pp. 337–55.
39. Leets, L., de Becker, G. and Giles, H. (1995) 'Fans: Exploring expressed motivations for contacting celebrities'. *Journal of Language and Social Psychology*, 14, pp. 102–24.
40. From George Kelly, *The Psychology of Personal Constructs*, Norton, 1955.
41. Gunter and McAleer, *Children and Television*, p. 47.
42. Cohen, J. and Metzger, M. 'Social affiliation', p. 54.
43. An interesting paper here is Silverstone, R. (1993) 'Television, ontological security and the transitional object'. *Media, Culture, and Society*, 15, pp. 573–98, which suggests that the parasocial relationships formed during childhood perform a similar function to a teddy or a security blanket, as 'transitional objects' that ease the separation of the infant from its mother. I suspect many of the cognitive processes involved in interaction with media figures are similar to those involved in attachments to cuddly toys and other inanimate objects in childhood. Certainly a degree of anthropomorphism is involved in both.
44. Rubin, A. M. and Rubin, R. B. (1985) 'Interface of personal and mediated communication: A research agenda'. *Critical Studies in Mass Communication*, 2, pp. 36–53.
45. Miller, R. V. (1983) 'A descriptive study of television usage among older Americans: Refining the parasocial concept'. Unpublished doctoral dissertation, Pennsylvania State University, University Park.

46. *Independent on Sunday*, 29 June 1997.
47. See James Weaver's chapter in Bryant, J. and Zillmann, D. (1991) *Responding to the Screen: Reception and Reaction Processes*. Hillsdale, NJ: Lawrence Erlbaum Associates. This is a comprehensive round-up of 'responses to erotica' studies. Typically, male undergraduates are 'exposed' to 'doses' of pornography and are asked to fill in a questionnaire before and after viewing, or asked to perform some other laboratory-based task (e.g., rating photos for attractiveness). The trend seems to be for viewers' post-experiment responses to be strongly guided by the content of the material they were 'exposed' to, thus producing a mish-mash of findings, only *some* of which are disturbing. Generalising from this type of research to 'real life' is a risky business!
48. Newton and Buck, 'Television as significant other'.
49. Doane, M. A. (1987) *The Desire to Desire: The Woman's Film of the 1940s*. Bloomington: Indiana University Press.
50. Oliver, M. B. (1993) 'Adolescents' enjoyment of graphic horror'. *Communication Research*, 20, pp. 30–50.
51. Davies, *Fake, Fact and Fantasy*.
52. Apter, M. J. (1982) *The Experience of Motivation: The Theory of psychological reversals*. San Diego: Academic Press.
53. Scannell (1996) contains some excellent archival research relating to British radio broadcasting in the 1940s.
54. Priest, P. J. (1995) *Public intimacies: Talk Show Participants and Tell-all TV*. Cresskill, NJ: Hampton. Similar research has been conducted in a British context by Sonia Livingstone and Peter Lunt (*Talk on Television: Audience Participation and Public Debate*. Routledge, 1994).
55. See Marshall (1997) Celebrity and Power: Fame in Contemporary Culture. Minneapolis: University of Minnesota Press.

5 Identity crises: the perils of 'authenticity'

1. Marshall, P. D. (1997) *Celebrity and Power: Fame in Contemporary Culture*. Minneapolis: University of Minnesota Press, 1997, p. 242.
2. Maybe there is some truth in this argument. It would probably take another whole book to deal with the topic in sufficient depth. However, it is almost impossible to prove that celebrity is solely a capitalist phenomenon because its emergence is so closely tied to technological development. Without film, television, and mass communications in general, there would be no celebrities. The fact that these technologies have emerged under capitalism may or may not be relevant – who can say? – but we can never separate the two.
3. Psychology as a discipline may owe its origins partly to capitalist desires to 'control' the masses (see Nikolas Rose's *Governing the*

Soul, Routledge, 1989). Once again, though, we are in the realms of historical determinism if we take this theory too seriously. As with the emergence of mass communications, a systematic study of private experiences may have evolved at any given time in any given culture – these things may be much more haphazard than Marxist historians would like to think.
4. Danziger, K. (1997) *Naming the Mind: How Psychology Found its Language*. London: Sage. It is possible that this separation of 'self' from 'world' was as much a product of urbanization as of the emergence of capitalism (and the positive connotations that 'self' would carry). Belief in one's pivotal role in some 'cosmic order' may have crumbled due to the sheer expansion of individual social networks and the awareness of one's relatively minor importance in the cosmos – ironically, a move *away* from egocentrism.
5. Geertz, C. (1979) 'From the native's point of view: On the nature of anthropological understanding'. In P. Rabinow and W. M. Sullivan (eds) *Interpretive Social Science*. Berkeley: University of California Press, pp. 225–41.
6. Sampson, E. (1989) 'The deconstruction of the self'. In J. Shotter and K. Gergen (eds) *Texts of Identity*. London: Sage, pp. 1–19.
7. Rose, *Governing the Soul*.
8. Ariès, P. (1962) *Centuries of Childhood: A Social History of Family Life* (R. Baldrick, trans.). New York: Random House.
9. Braudy, L. (1997) *The Frency of Renown: Fame and its History* (2nd edition). New York: Vintage Books.
10. Gergen, K. J. (1991) *The Saturated Self*. New York: Basic Books.
11. Rogers, C. (1961) *On Becoming a Person*. Boston: Houghton Mifflin.
12. Maslow, A. H. (1968) *Towards a Psychology of Being*. New York: Van Nostrand.
13. The problem with this approach is that it is far from unitary! I recommend Rom Harré and Grant Gillett's *The Discursive Mind* (Sage, 1994) as a readable introduction. I have published some work myself on the discursive construction of identity, although in a broader context looking at the phenomenon of drunkenness: Giles, D. (1999) 'Retrospective accounts of drunken behaviour: implications for theories of self, memory and the discursive construction of identity'. *Discourse Studies*, 1(4).
14. An example is Blasi, A. and Milton, K. (1991) 'The development of the sense of self in adolescence'. *Journal of Personality*, 59, pp. 217–39. I have no particular objection to this type of research, though the original models are highly culture-bound.
15. Markus, H. R. and Kityama, S. (1991) 'Culture and the self: Implications for cognition, emotion and motivation'. *Psychological Review*, **98**, pp. 224–53.

16. Triandis, H. C. (1995) *Individualism and Collectivism*. Boulder, CO: Westview.
17. Lay, C., Fairlie, P., Jackson, S., Ricci, T., Eisenberg, J., Sato, T., Teeäär, A. and Melamud, A. (1998). 'Domain-specific allocentrism-idiocentrism'. *Journal of Cross-Cultural Psychology*, **29**, pp. 434–60.
18. Cross, S. E. and Madson, L. (1997a) 'Models of the self: Self-construals and gender'. *Psychological Bulletin*, **122**, pp. 5–37.
19. Clancy, S. M. and Dollinger, S. J. (1993) 'Photographic depictions of the self: Gender and age differences in social connectedness'. *Sex Roles*, **29**, pp. 477–95.
20. Cross, S. E. and Madson, L. (1997b) 'Elaboration of models of the self: Reply to Baumeister and Sommer (1997) and Martin and Ruble (1997)'. *Psychological Bulletin*, **122**, pp. 51–5.
21. Part of the problem may lie in the perceived need to develop 'instruments' for 'measuring' the sense of self. A typical self-construal scale consists of items like 'I act the same way no matter who I am with' which respondents are asked to agree or disagree with using a Likert scale (say, 1–7). Such scales are hugely susceptible to the effects of 'social desirability', which makes them intrinsically culture-bound (for example, Americans are more likely to agree with highly 'independent' items while British respondents feel obliged to be modest). Therefore the instrument may not be a measure of private experience so much as a reflection of cultural perspectives on self; ideal for cross-cultural purposes then, but useless for an individual psychology.
22. Vonk, R. and Ashmore, R. D. (1993) 'The multifaceted self: Androgyny reassessed by open-ended self-descriptions'. *Social Psychology Quarterly*, **56**, 278–87.
23. Harré, R. (1983) *Personal Being*. Cambridge, MA: Harvard University Press.
24. Harré and Gillett, *The Discursive Mind*.
25. The concept of 'true self' possibly derives from the work of the British psychoanalyst D.W. Winnicott (*The Maturational Processes and the Facilitating Environment*, The Hogarth Press, 1965). Winnicott argued that the concept of true self emerges during adolescence, when one becomes conscious of the different masks one has to don in order to progress toward adulthood, and feelings of authenticity and sincerity also develop. The question remains: where does this 'true' self come from – parental upbringing? Genetic uniqueness? Or social convention? (Cross-cultural researchers would, perhaps, argue that individuals in other cultures are perfectly happy to present a multiplicity of 'selves' without ever feeling compromised.)
26. Schaller, M. (1997) 'The psychological consequences of fame: Three tests of the self-consciousness hypothesis'. *Journal of Personality*, **65**, pp. 291–309.

27. Frith, D. (1991) *By his own hand: A study of cricket's suicides*. London: Stanley Paul. Cricket seems to have more than its fair share of suicides, perhaps because the nature of the sport requires a high degree of self-absorption for success and, unlike British football, the opportunities for perpetuating fame afterwards, in club management or punditry, are somewhat limited.
28. Simonton, D. K. (1994) *Greatness: Who Makes History and Why*. New York: Guildford Press.
29. Braudy (1997) *The Frency of Renown*
30. Ibid., p. 29.
31. A copy of Kurt Cobain's suicide note is accessible via the internet address *http://www.pcuf.fi/~diddle/nirvana/Nirvana_Note.html*
32. Dyer, R. (1991) 'A Star is Born and the construction of authenticity'. In C. Gledhill (ed.) *Stardom: Industry of desire*. London: Routledge, p. 133.
33. Ibid., p. 139.
34. *Melody Maker*, 13 January 1996.
35. Giddens, A. (1991) *Modernity and Self-identity: Self and Society in the Late Modern Age*. Cambridge: Polity Press.
36. *Guardian*, 15 June 1991.
37. Negus, K. (1992) *Producing Pop: Culture and Conflict in the Popular Music Industry*. London: Edward Arnold, p. 117.
38. Brando, M. and Lindsey, R. (1994) *Brando: Songs My Mother Taught Me*. London: Century.
39. *Guardian*, 9 April 1995.
40. *Q* magazine, September 1993.
41. Adler, P. A. and Adler, P. (1989) 'The glorified self: The aggrandizement and the constriction of self'. *Social Psychology Quarterly*, 52, pp. 299–310.
42. Ibid., p. 304.
43. *Q* magazine, November 1993.
44. *Independent on Sunday*, 25 October 1992.
45. Gergen, *The Saturated Self*, p. 205.
46. Brand, G. and Scannell, P. (1991) 'Talk, identity and performance: The Tony Blackburn show'. In P. Scannell (ed.) *Broadcast Talk*. London: Sage, pp. 201–26.
47. Tolson, A. (1991) 'Televised chat and the synthetic personality'. In P. Scannell (ed.) *Broadcast Talk*. London: Sage, pp. 178–200.

6 The problems of being famous

1. Swenson, K. (1997) *Greta Garbo: A Life Apart*. New York: Scribner.
2. Ibid., pp. 264–5.
3. Chaplin, C. (1964) *My Autobiography*. London: The Bodley Head.

4. Ibid., p. 289.
5. Ibid., p. 190.
6. *Independent*, 31 May 1994.
7. Braudy, L. (1997) *The Frenzy of Renown: Fame and its History* (2nd edition). New York: Vintage Books.
8. Gergen, K. J. (1991) *The Saturated Self*. New York: Basic Books, p. 62.
9. Milardo, R. (1992) 'Comparative methods for delineating social networks'. *Journal of Social and Personal Relationships*, **9**, pp. 447–61.
10. Milardo, R., Johnson, M. P. and Huston, T. (1983) 'Developing close relationships'. *Journal of Personality and Social Psychology*, **44**, pp. 964–76.
11. For example, one method employed to this end involves a highly dubious sampling technique where names are randomly selected from a telephone directory and participants are asked how many people with those names form part of their global networks. The total is then adjusted according to the number of entries in the local directory. The estimate (in North America) is 1700, plus or minus 400 (Killworth, P. D., Johnsen, E. C., Bernard, H. R., Shelley, G. A. and McCarty, C. (1990) 'Estimating the size of personal networks'. *Social Networks*, **12**, pp. 289–312).
12. Again, there is a lack of research in what types of acquaintance constitute an individual's 'global network'. What does 'knowing' someone involve? A distinction is needed, perhaps, between people whom one gets to know during the course of one's everyday interaction, and people familiar through other media. However, the emergence of communication media such as e-mail means that some degree of 'virtuality' needs to be considered even at the level of interactive networks. Another issue is that, as I have argued earlier, we can become famous *locally* without much media assistance, so the 'known to' network need not be virtual in nature. Clearly there is plenty of scope for developing this research area.
13. *Q* magazine, June 1992.
14. *The Sunday Times*, 13 October 1996.
15. *Independent* 4 October 1996.
16. *Independent*, 14 June 1992.
17. *Q* magazine, November 1989.
18. Perlman, D. and Peplau, L. A. (1981) 'Toward a social psychology of loneliness'. In S. W. Duck and R. Gilmour (eds) *Personal Relationships 3: Personal Relationships in Disorder*. London: Academic Press.
19. Braudy, ibid., p. 79.
20. Ibid., p. 373.
21. Davies, R. (ed.) (1993) *The Kenneth Williams Diaries*. London: HarperCollins. Date of entry: 25 February 1973.
22. *Melody Maker*, 3 August 1996

NOTES AND REFERENCES 171

23. Cited in Westin, A. (1970) *Privacy and Freedom*. New York: Atheneum, pp. 16–17).
24. Altman, I. (1975) *The Environment and Social Behaviour: Privacy, Personal Space, Territoriality and Overcrowding*. Monterrey, CA: Brooks and Cole.
25. Ariès, P. (1962) *Centuries of Childhood: A Social History of Family Life* (R. baldrik, trans.). New York: Random House.
26. Braudy, Ibid.
27. There is a growing literature on the significance of the private bedroom in adolescence. An early reference is Parke, R. and Sawin, D. (1979) 'Children's privacy in the home: Developmental, ecological and child-rearing determinants'. *Environment and Behavior*, 11, pp. 87–104. More recently, the *Journal of Youth and Adolescence* devoted a special issue to the use of media within the context of the private bedroom (Volume 24(5), 1995), and the *Journal of Family Issues* has recently run a special issue on the subject of children's privacy in the home (January 1998). As this book goes to press, I am in the process of conducting a study investigating how one's sense of self may be affected by sharing (or not sharing) a bedroom in childhood; pilot findings suggest that 'sharers' may display a more interdependent view of self (though the study at present suffers from the same constraints as I mentioned when discussing the literature on self-construal in Chapter 5).
28. *Independent*, 29 September 1997.
29. *Q magazine*, June 1992.
30. *Guardian*, 17 July 1990.
31. Marshall, P. D. (1997) *Celebrity and Power: Fame in Contemporary Culture*. Mineapolis: University of Minnesota Press, p. 134.
32. *Q magazine*, March 1989.
33. Much, N. and Mahapatra, M. (1995) 'Constructing divinity'. In R. Harré and P. Stearns (eds.) *Discursive Psychology in Practice*. London: Sage.
34. Ibid., p. 60.
35. Ibid., p. 68.
36. Ibid., p. 71.
37. *Q magazine*, November 1989.
38. *Q magazine*, September 1993.
39. *Melody Maker*, 21 May 1994.
40. Gamson, J. (1994) *Claims to Fame: Celebrity in Contemporary America*: University of California Press.
41. *Melody Maker*, 21 May 1994.
42. *The Times*, 8 April 1995.
43. Davies, *The Kenneth Williams Diaries*. Date of entry: Sunday 4 April 1971.

44. Ibid. Date of entry: 28 February 1975.
45. *Guardian*, 17 March 1996.

7 A taxonomy of fame

1. Braudy, L. (1997) *The Frenzy of Renown: Fame and its History* (2nd edition). New York: Vintage Books.
2. A number of fellow academics have suggested taxonomies of modern celebrities which are based on activities. For instance, Mark Griffiths (personal communication) has argued for a typology comprising public office, sport, entertainment, professions (e.g., psychology, law, journalism) and crime/infamy. While such a typology is more intuitive than the one described here (and easier to build upon, since one can just keep adding categories over time), my intention was to create a typology that reflected the process of fame, and such a system would require quite broad categories. The problem with activity-based typologies, as I see it, is that they can be broken down into an infinite number of sub-categories – for example, 'sport' embraces as wide a variety of different fame experiences as 'entertainment', partly through the different routes by which individuals in these areas achieve fame, and this heterogeneity would need to be reflected in a model.
3. Braudy, ibid., p. 84.
4. Ibid., p. 234.
5. Pop music is a notoriously difficult domain in which to establish any sort of meritocracy. Reed Larson ('Secrets in the bedroom: Adolescents' private use of media'. *Journal of Youth and Adolescence*, 1995, **24**, pp. 535–50) has found that teenagers spent more time engaged with the media when alone than when in the company of their peers. I would suggest that, for this reason, 'taste' in popular music (typically formed during adolescence) is, for most people, an intensely private matter, and is subject to much higher variance than tastes and preferences in more communal activities. Another factor is that, unlike films or television, music is very open to subjective interpretation, something which is acknowledged by the convention of 'our tune' (i.e., certain records hold sentimental value to romantic partners). Therefore, meanings may be attached to a piece of music for one listener which are indecipherable to another.
6. Martindale, C. (1990) *The Clockwork Muse: The Predictability of Artistic Change*. New York: Basic Books.
7. Cited in Simonton, D. K. (1994) *Greatness: Who Makes History and Why*. New York: Guildford Press.

8. Gledhill C. (ed.) (1991) *Stardom: Industry of Desire*. London: Routledge.
9. Griffiths, M. and Joinson, A. (1998) 'Max-imum impact: The psychology of fame'. *Psychology Post*, 6, pp. 8–9.
10. Braudy, ibid.
11. See Moran, J. (1998) 'Cultural Studies and Academic Stardom'. *International Journal of Cultural Studies*, 1, pp. 67–82.
12. Simonton, D. K. (1997) 'Career productivity: A predictive and explanatory model of career trajectories and landmarks'. *Psychological Review*, 104, pp. 66–89.

8 Beyond parasocial interaction: fans and stalkers

1. Yano, C. (1997) 'Charisma's realm: Fandom in Japan'. *Ethnology*, 36, pp. 335–49.
2. Braudy, L. (1997) *The Frency of Renown: Fame and its History* (2nd edition). New York: Vintage Books.
3. Ibid., p. 381.
4. Jenkins, H. (1992) *Textual Poachers: Television Fans and Participatory Culture*. New York: Routledge.
5. Gamson, J. (1994) *Claims to Fame: Celebrating in Contemporary America*. University of California Press.
6. Ibid., p. 54.
7. Ibid., p. 183.
8. Jenkins, *Textual Poachers*.
9. See also Jenson, J. (1992) 'Fandom as pathology: The consequences of characterization'. In L. Lewis (ed.) *The Adoring Audience: Fan Culture and Popular Media*. London: Routledge.
10. Ibid., p. 23.
11. However, I have collected some interesting interview data recently that seems to support Gamson's argument, from female soap fans who claim that bad acting makes them engage less with characters (i.e., weakens the parasocial interaction). Awareness of the techniques of simulacrum, or 'seeing the strings', does not seem to impair fans' engagement with soap as a genre.
12. Garratt, S. (1990), 'Signed, Sealed and Delivered'. In S. Frith and A. Goodwin (eds) *On Record: Rock, Pop and the Written Word*. London: Routledge.
13. Ibid., p. 410.
14. Ibid., p. 404.
15. Ibid., p. 409.
16. Hornby, N. (1992) *Fever Pitch*. London: Victor Gollancz, pp. 194–5.
17. Jewett, R. and Lawrence J. S. (1977) *The American monomyth*. Garden City, NewYork: Anchor/Doubleday, cited in Jenkins, *Textual Poachers*.

18. Braudy, ibid.
19. Jindra, M. (1994) 'Star Trek fandom as a religious phenomenon'. *Sociology of Religion*, 55, pp. 27–51.
20. Much, N. and Mahapatra, M. (1994) 'Constructing divinity'. In R. Harré and P. Stearns (eds) *Discursive Psychology in Practice*. London: Sage, p. 60.
21. Vermorel, F. and Vermorel, J. (1990) 'Last words: The fans speak'. In S. Frith and A. Goodwin (eds) *On Record: Rock, Pop and the Written Word*. London: Routledge, pp. 481–90. Also see Vermorel, F. and Vermorel, J. (1985) *Starlust: The Secret Fantasies of Fans*. London: W. H. Allen.
22. Vermorel and Vermorel, 1990, *Starlust*, p. 484.
23. Jaynes, J. (1976) *The Origin of Consciousness in the Breakdown of the Bicameral Mind*. London: Penguin.
24. Tudor, A. (1974) *Image and Influence: Studies in the Sociology of Film*. London: George Allen & Unwin, p. 82.
25. Vermorel & Vermorel, *Starlust*, p. 488.
26. Tudor, *Image and Influence*, p. 83.
27. Hardy, T. (1896) *Jude the Obscure*. Pan Books, p. 200.
28. *Independent on Sunday*, 29 June 1997.
29. *Observer*, 14 June 1998.
30. Garratt, 'Signed, sealed and delivered'.
31. Dietz, P. E., Matthews, D. B., Van Duyne, C., Martell, D. A., Parry, C. D. H., Stewart, T., Warren, J. and Crowder, J. D. (1991) 'Threatening and otherwise inappropriate letters to Hollywood celebrities'. *Journal of Forensic Sciences*, 36, pp. 185–209.
32. The full list is included in the Dietz *et al.* (1991) article, although few of the items are discussed in the text, and this leaves their significance open to all manner of interpretation. For example, it is not disclosed whether or not the blood in the syringe was tested (was it, for example, HIV-positive?). Most obscure of all is the item 'a motorcycle', hardly the sort of thing you would expect to fall out of an envelope.
33. Leets, L., De Becker, G. and Giles, H. (1995) 'Fans: Exploring expressed motivations for contacting celebrities'. *Journal of Language and Social Psychology*, 14, pp. 102–24.
34. Cited in Franzini, L. R. and Grossberg, J. M. (1995) *Eccentric and Bizarre Behaviors*. New York: John Wiley.
35. *The Sunday Times*, 28 June 1998.

9 Postscript: the future of celebrity

1. Neuman, W. R. (1991) *The Future of the Mass Audience*. Cambridge University Press.

2. Cantril, H. & Allport, G. (1935) *The Psychology of Radio*. New York: Harper & Brothers.
3. Hald, A. P. (1982) 'Toward an information-rich society'. In E. Cornish (ed.) *Communications Tomorrow*. Bethesda, MD: World Future Society, p. 11.
4. Arterton, F. C. (1987) *Teledemocracy: Can Technology Protect Democracy?* Newbury Park, CA: Sage.
5. Alas, people who find themselves at the 'sharp end' of technology use – the Luddites, for instance – are rarely consulted when management decides to make a change. Even in higher education, academics find themselves under pressure to deliver 'distance learning packages' and develop 'virtual' teaching methods despite few of us, other than educationalists, displaying much enthusiasm for the current mania for computerizing everything computerizable!
6. Neuman, *The Future of the Mass Audience*.
7. Steemers, J. (1997) 'Broadcasting is dead. Long live digital choice: Perspectives from the United Kingdom and Germany'. *Convergence*, **3**, pp. 51–71.
8. Scannell, P. and Cardiff, P. (1991) *A Social History of British Broadcasting*. Oxford: Blackwell.
9. Mitra, A. (1997) 'Diasporic web sites: Ingroup and outgroup discourse'. *Critical Studies in Mass Communication*, **14**, pp. 158–81. This paper describes how ethnic groups from the Indian subcontinent have established internet communities across the world.
10. Shapiro, M. A. and McDonald, D. G. (1995) 'I'm not a real doctor, but I play one in virtual reality: Implications of virtual reality for judgments about reality'. In F. Biocca and M. R. Levy (eds,) *Communication in the Age of Virtual Reality*. Hillsdale, NJ: Lawrence Erlbaum Associates, p. 331.
11. Ibid., p. 336.
12. Winston, B. (1998) *Media, Technology and Society – A History: From the Telegraph to the Internet*. London: Routledge.
13. Turkle, S. (1995) *Life on the Screen: Identity in the Age of the Internet*. New York: Simon & Schuster.
14. A recent reference here is Gackenbach, J. (ed.)(1998) *Psychology and the Internet*. Academic Press, which contains plenty of material concerning gender, self and consciousness, among other themes.
15. Drees, D. (1998) 'The mystery of relationships by e-mail'. Paper presented at the Annual Conference of the British Psychological Society's Student Members Group, Brighton Conference Centre, 28 March.
16. Winston, *Media, Technology and Society*.
17. Ibid., p. 336.

Appendix

1. Too numerous to list here! Vicki Bruce is the leading British (and world?) expert on face recognition, and has written numerous books and papers on the topic, and Tim Valentine has integrated some of her work into his own research on the cognitive psychology of proper names. Famous names often feature as stimuli in neuropsychological studies, though as dependent rather than independent variables. Nevertheless, there may be some interesting phenomena arising from this type of research for cognitive perspectives on the topic of fame and celebrity.

Bibliography

Adler, A. (1938) *Social Interest* (J. Linton and R. Vaughan, trans.). London: Faber & Faber.
Adler, P. A. and Adler, P. (1989), 'The glorified self: the aggrandizement and the constriction of self'. *Social Psychology Quarterly*, **52**, pp. 299–310.
Altman, I. (1975) *The Environment and Social Behaviour: Privacy, Personal Space, Territoriality and Overcrowding*. Monterrey, Ca: Brooks and Cole.
Apter, M. J. (1982) *The Experience of Motivation: The Theory of Psychological Reversals*. San Diego: Academic Press.
Ariès, P. (1962) *Centuries of Childhood: A Social History of Family Life* (R. Baldrick, trans.). New York: Random House.
Arterton, F. C. (1987) *Teledemocracy: Can Technology Protect Democracy?* Newbury Park, CA: Sage.
Baker, R. (1996) *Sperm Wars: Infidelity, Sexual Conflict and Other Bedroom Battles*. London: Fourth Estate.
Barker, M. and Petley, J. (1997) *Ill Effects: The Media/Violence Debate*. London: Routledge.
Bianculli, D. (1992) *Tele-literacy: Taking Television Seriously*. New York: Continuum.
Blasi, A. and Milton, K. (1991) 'The development of the sense of self in adolescence'. *Journal of Personality*, 59, pp. 217–39.
Boorstin, D. J. (1961) *The Image: A Guide to Pseudo-events in America*. New York: Harper and Row.
Brando, M. and Lindsey, R. (1994) *Brando: Songs My Mother Taught Me*. London: Century.
Braudy, L. (1997) *The Frenzy of Renown: Fame and its History* (2nd edition). New York: Vintage Books.
Bryant, J. and Zillmann, D. (eds) (1991) *Responding to the Screen: Reception and Reaction Processes*. Lawrence Erlbaum Associates.
Cantril, H. and Allport, G. (1935) *The Psychology of Radio*. New York: Harper and Brothers.
Cashmore, E. (1994) *... And then there was television*. London: Routledge.
Chaplin, C. (1964) *My autobiography*. London: The Bodley Head.
Charlton, T. , Coles, D. and Lovemore, T. (1997) 'Teachers' ratings of nursery class children's behaviour before and after availability of television by satellite'. *Psychological Reports*, **81**, pp. 96–8.

Chaucer, G. (1957) *The Works of Geoffrey Chaucer* (2nd edition). London University Press.
Cicero, M. T. (45 BC, 1943) 'Tusculan disputations'. In J. E. King (trans.) *Cicero in twenty eight volumes, No. 18*. London: William Heinemann.
Clancy, S. M. and Dollinger, S. J. (1993) 'Photographic depictions of the self: Gender and age differences in social connectedness'. *Sex Roles*, **29**, pp. 477–95.
Clark, R. W. (1980) *Freud*. New York: Random House.
Cohen, J. and Metzger, M. (1998) 'Social affiliation and the achievement of ontological security through interpersonal and mass communication'. *Critical Studies in Mass Communication*, **15**, pp. 41–60.
Comstock, G. , Chaffee, S. , Katzman, N. , McCombs, M. and Roberts, D. (1978) *Television and Human Behaviour*. Columbia University Press.
Cortez, C. A. (1992) 'Mediated interpersonal communication: The role of attraction and perceived homophily in the development of parasocial relationships'. Doctoral dissertation, University of Iowa.
Cross, S. E. and Madson, L. (1997a) 'Models of the self: Self-construals and gender. *Psychological Bulletin*, **122**, pp. 5–37.
Cross, S. E. and Madson, L. (1997b) 'Elaboration of models of the self: Reply to Baumeister and Sommer (1997) and Martin and Ruble (1997)'. *Psychological Bulletin*, **122**, pp. 51–5.
Dante Alighieri (1955) *The Comedy of Dante Alighieri, the Florentine: Cantica 2: Purgatory (Il Purgatorio)*, trans. D. L. Sayers. London: Penguin.
Danziger, K. (1997) *Naming the Mind: How Psychology Found its Language*. London: Sage.
Davies, M. M. (1997) *Fake, Fact and Fantasy: Children's Interpretations of Television Reality*. Mahwah, NJ: Lawrence Erlbaum Associates.
Davies, R. (ed.) (1993) *The Kenneth Williams Diaries*. London: HarperCollins.
Dawkins, R. (1976/1989) *The Selfish Gene*. Oxford University Press.
Dietz, P. E. , Matthews, D. B. , Van Duyne, C. , Martell, D. A. , Parry, C. D. H. , Stewart, T. , Warren, J. and Crowder, J. D. (1991) 'Threatening and otherwise inappropriate letters to Hollywood celebrities'. *Journal of Forensic Sciences*, **36**, pp. 185–209.
Doane, M. A. (1987) *The Desire to Desire: The Woman's Film of the 1940s*. Bloomington: Indiana University Press.
Edwards, D. (1996) *Discourse and Cognition*. London: Sage.
Erikson, E. H. (1950) *Childhood and Society*. New York: Norton.
Foucault, M. (1981) *The History of Sexuality*, Vol. 1. Penguin.
Franzini, L. R. and Grossberg, J. M. (1995) *Eccentric and Bizarre Behaviors*. New York: John Wiley.
Frith, D. (1991) *By His Own Hand: A Study of Cricket's Suicides*. London: Stanley Paul.
Frith, S. and Goodwin, A. (eds) (1990) *On Record: Rock, Pop and the Written Word*. London: Routledge.

Gackenbach, J. (ed.) (1998) *Psychology and the Internet*. Academic Press.
Gamson, J. (1994) *Claims to Fame: Celebrity in Contemporary America*. University of California Press.
Gedo, J. E. (1996) *The Artist and the Emotional World*. New York: Columbia University Press.
Geertz, C. (1979) 'From the native's point of view: On the nature of anthropological understanding'. In P. Rabinow and W. M. Sullivan (eds) *Interpretive Social Science*. Berkeley: University of California Press, pp. 225–41.
Gergen, K. J. (1991) *The Saturated Self*. New York: Basic Books.
Giddens, A. (1991) *Modernity and Self-identity: Self and Society in the Late Modern Age*. Cambridge: Polity Press.
Giles, D. (1999) 'Retrospective accounts of drunken behaviour: implications for theories of self, memory and the discursive construction of identity'. *Discourse Studies*, 1(4).
Gledhill, C. (ed) (1991) *Stardom: Industry of Desire*. London: Routledge.
Granzberg, G. (1985) 'Television and self-concept formation in developing areas: The central Canadian Algonkian experience'. *Journal of Cross Cultural Psychology*, **16**, p. 323.
Griffiths, M. and Joinson, A. (1998) 'Max-imum impact: The psychology of fame'. *Psychology Post*, **6**, 8–9.
Gunter, B. (1987) *Poor Reception: Misunderstanding and Forgetting Broadcast News*. Hillsdale, NJ: Lawrence Erlbaum Associates.
Gunter, B. and McAleer, J. (1997) *Children and Television* (2nd edition). London: Routledge.
Hald, A. P. (1982) 'Toward an information-rich society'. In E. Cornish (ed.) *Communications Tomorrow*. Bethesda, MD: World Future Society.
Hardy, T. (1896) *Jude the obscure*. Pan Books.
Harré, R. (1983) *Personal Being*. Cambridge, MA: Harvard University Press.
Harré, R. and Gillett, G. (1994) *The Discursive Mind*. London: Sage.
Harris, R. J. (1991) *The Cognitive Psychology of Mass Communication*. Hillsdale, NJ: Lawrence Erlbaum Associates.
Harvey, D. (1990) *The Condition of Postmodernity*. Cambridge, MA: Blackwell.
Healey, D. (1989) *The Time of My Life*. London: Penguin.
Himmelweit, H. T., Oppenheim, A. N. and Vince, P. (1958) *Television and the child*. London: Oxford University Press.
Hodge, B. and Tripp, D. (1986) *Children and Television*. Cambridge: Polity Press.
Hornby, N. (1992) *Fever Pitch*. London: Victor Gollancz.
Horton, D. and Wohl, R. R. (1956) 'Mass communication and para-social interaction'. *Psychiatry*, **19**, pp. 215–229.
Jamison, K. R. (1989) 'Mood disorders and patterns of creativity in British writers and artists'. *Psychiatry*, **52**, 125–34.

Jaynes, J. (1976, 1990) *The Origin of Consciousness in the Breakdown of the Bicameral Mind*. London: Penguin.
Jenkins, H. (1992) *Textual Poachers: Television Fans and Participatory Culture*. New York: Routledge.
Jenson, J. (1992) 'Fandom as pathology: The consequences of characterization'. In L. Lewis (ed.) *The Adoring Audience: Fan Culture and Popular Media*. London: Routledge.
Jindra, M. (1994) 'Star Trek fandom as a religious phenomenon'. *Sociology of Religion*, **55**, pp. 27–51.
Killworth, P. D. , Johnsen, E. C. , Bernard, H. R. , Shelley, G. A. and McCarty, C. (1990) 'Estimating the size of personal networks'. *Social Networks*, **12**, pp. 289–312.
Kotre, J. (1996) *Outliving the Self: How We Live on in Future Generations*. New York: W. W. Norton.
Kubey, R. and Csikszentmihalyi, M. (1990) *Television and the Quality of Life: How Viewing Shapes Everyday Experience*. Hillsdale, NJ: Lawrence Erlbaum Associates.
Larson, R. (1995) 'Secrets in the bedroom: Adolescents' private use of media'. *Journal of Youth and Adolescence*, **24**, pp. 535–50.
Lay, C. , Fairlie, P. , Jackson, S. , Ricci, T. , Eisenberg, J. , Sato, T. , Teeäär, A. and Melamud, A. (1998) 'Domain-specific allocentrism-idiocentrism'. *Journal of Cross-Cultural Psychology*, **29**, pp. 434–60.
Leets, L. , de Becker, G. and Giles, H. (1995) 'Fans: Exploring expressed motivations for contacting celebrities'. *Journal of Language and Social Psychology*, **14**, pp. 102–24.
Livingstone, S. and Lunt, P. (1994) *Talk on Television: Audience Participation and Public Debate*. London: Routledge.
Markus, H. R. and Kityama, S. (1991) 'Culture and the self: Implications for cognition, emotion and motivation'. *Psychological Review*, **98**, pp. 224–53.
Marshall, P. D. (1997) *Celebrity and Power: Fame in Contemporary Culture*. Minneapolis: University of Minnesota Press.
Martindale, C. (1990) *The Clockwork Muse: The Predictability of Artistic Change*. New York: Basic Books.
Maslow, A. H. (1968) *Towards a Psychology of Being*. New York: Van Nostrand.
McAdams, D. P. (1985) *Power, Intimacy and the Life Story: Personological Inquiries into Identity*. New York: Guilford Press.
McAdams, D. P. and de St. Aubin, E. (1992) 'A theory of generativity and its assessment through self-report, behavioral acts, and narrative themes in autobiography'. *Journal of Personality and Social Psychology*, **62**, pp. 1003–15.
Milardo, R. (1992) 'Comparative methods for delineating social networks'. *Journal of Social and Personal Relationships*, 9, pp. 447–61.

Milardo, R. , Johnson, M. P. and Huston, T. (1983) 'Developing close relationships'. *Journal of Personality and Social Psychology*, **44**, pp. 964–76.
Miller, R. V. (1983) 'A descriptive study of television usage among older Americans: Refining the parasocial concept'. Unpublished doctoral dissertation, Pennsylvania State University, University Park.
Milton, J. (1989) *Paradise Lost*, trans. C. Ricks. London: Penguin.
Mitra, A. (1997) 'Diasporic web sites: Ingroup and outgroup discourse'. *Critical Studies in Mass Communication*, **14**, pp. 158–81.
Moran, J. (1998) 'Cultural studies and academic stardom'. *International Journal of Cultural Studies*, **1**, pp. 67–82.
Much, N. and Mahapatra, M. (1995) 'Constructing divinity'. In R Harré and P. Stearns (eds) *Discursive Psychology in Practice*. London: Sage.
Negus, K. (1992) *Producing Pop: Culture and Conflict in the Popular Music Industry*. London: Edward Arnold.
Neuman, W. R. (1991) *The Future of the Mass Audience*. Cambridge University Press.
Newhagen, J. E. and Reeves, B. (1992) 'The evening's bad news: Effects of compelling negative television news imagery'. *Journal of Communication*, **42**, pp. 25–41.
Newton, A. J. and Buck, E. B. (1985) 'Television as significant other: Its relationship to self-descriptors in five developing countries'. *Journal of Cross Cultural Psychology*, **16**, pp. 289–312.
Noble, G. (1975) *Children in front of the small screen*. Beverly Hills, CA: Sage.
Oliver, M. B. (1993) 'Adolescents' enjoyment of graphic horror'. *Communication Research*, **20**, pp. 30–50.
**Paget, D. (1998) *No other way to tell it: Dramadoc/docudrama on telelvision*. Manchester: Manchester University Press.
Parke, R. and Sawin, D. (1979) 'Children's privacy in the home: Developmental, ecological and child-rearing determinants'. *Environment and Behavior*, **11**, pp. 87–104.
Parker, I. (1992). *Discourse Dynamics: Critical Analysis for Social and Individual Psychology*. London: Routledge.
Pearson, J. (1995). *The Profession of Violence: The Rise and Fall of the Kray Twins* (4th edition). London: HarperCollins.
Perlman, D. and Peplau, L. A. (1981) 'Toward a social psychology of loneliness'. In S. W. Duck and R. Gilmour (eds) *Personal relationships 3: Personal relationships in disorder*. London: Academic Press.
Picirillo, M. S. (1986) 'On the authenticity of televisual experience: A critical exploration of parasocial closure'. *Critical Studies in Mass Communication*, **3**, pp. 337–55.
Priest, P. J. (1995) *Public intimacies: Talk show participants and tell-all TV*. Cresskill, NJ: Hampton.

Reeves, B. and Nass, C. (1996) *The Media Equation: How People Treat Computers, Television, and New Media like Real People and Places*. Stanford University: Cambridge University Press.

Reynolds, S. (1990) *Blissed Out: The Raptures of Rock*. London: Serpent's Tail.

Rice, M. L. , Huston, A. C. and Wright, J. C. (1983) 'The forms of television: Effects on children's attention, comprehension, and social behaviour'. In M. Meyer (ed.) *Children and the Formal Features of Television: Approaches and Findings of Experimental and Formative Research*. Munich: K. G. Saur.

Rogan, J. (1992) *Morrissey and Marr: The Severed Alliance*. London: Omnibus.

Rogers, C. (1961) *On Becoming a Person*. Boston: Houghton Mifflin.

Rose, N. (1989) *Governing the Soul*. London: Routledge.

Rose, S. , Lewontin, R. C. and Kamin, L. J. (1984) *Not in our Genes: Biology, Ideology and Human Nature*. London: Penguin.

Rubin, R. B. and McHugh, M. P. (1987) 'Development of parasocial interaction relationships'. *Journal of Broadcasting and Electronic Media*, **31**, pp. 279–92.

Rubin, A. M. , Perse, E. M. , and Powell, R. A. (1985) 'Loneliness, parasocial interaction, and local television news viewing'. *Human Communication Research*, **12**, pp. 155–80.

Rubin, A. M. and Rubin, R. B. (1985) 'Interface of personal and mediated communication: A research agenda'. *Critical Studies in Mass Communication*, **2**, pp. 36–53.

Sampson, E. (1989) 'The deconstruction of the self'. In J. Shotter and K. Gergen (eds) *Texts of Identity*. London: Sage, pp. 1–19.

Samuels, A. and Taylor, M. (1994) 'Children's ability to distinguish fantasy events from real-life events'. *British Journal of Developmental Psychology*, **12**, pp. 417–27.

Sandeen, C. (1997) 'Success defined by television: The value system promoted by *PM* magazine'. *Critical Studies in Mass Communication*, **14**, pp. 77–105.

Scannell, P. (ed.) (1991) *Broadcast Talk*. London: Sage.

Scannell, P. (1996) *Radio, Television and Modern Life*. Oxford: Blackwell.

Scannell, P. and Cardiff, D. (1991) *A Social History of British Broadcasting*. Oxford: Blackwell.

Schaller, M. (1997) 'The psychological consequences of fame: Three tests of the self-consciousness hypothesis'. *Journal of Personality*, **65**, pp. 291–309.

Shapiro, M. A. and McDonald, D. G. (1995) 'I'm not a real doctor, but I play one in virtual reality: Implications of virtual reality for judgments about reality'. In F. Biocca and M. R. Levy (eds) *Communication in the Age of Virtual Reality*. Hillsdale, NJ: Lawrence Erlbaum Associates, pp. 323–45.

Silverstone, R. (1993) 'Television, ontological security and the transitional object'. *Media, Culture, and Society,* **15**, pp. 573–98.
Simonton, D. K. (1994) *Greatness: Who Makes History and Why.* New York: The Guilford Press.
Simonton, D. K. (1997) 'Career productivity: A predictive and explanatory model of career trajectories and landmarks'. *Psychological Review,* **104**, pp. 66–89.
Steemers, J. (1997) 'Broadcasting is dead. Long live digital choice: Perspectives from the United Kingdom and Germany'. *Convergence,* **3**, pp. 51–71.
Swenson, K. (1997) *Greta Garbo: A Life Apart.* New York: Scribner.
Tagg, J. (1988) *The Burden of Representation: Essays on Photographies and Histories.* Basingstoke: Macmillan.
Taraborelli, J. R. (1992) *Michael Jackson: The Magic and the Madness.* New York: Ballantine.
Thomson, R. G. (ed.) (1996) *Freakery: Cultural Spectacles of the Extraordinary Body.* New York University Press.
Triandis, H. C. (1995) *Individualism and Collectivism.* Boulder, CO: Westview.
Tudor, A. (1974) *Image and Influence: Studies in the Sociology of Film.* London: George Allen and Unwin.
Turkle, S. (1995) *Life on the Screen: Identity in the Age of the Internet.* New York: Simon and Schuster.
Vermorel, F. and Vermorel, J. (1985) *Starlust: The Secret Fantasies of Fans.* London: W. H. Allen.
Vonk, R. and Ashmore, R. D. (1993) 'The multifaceted self: Androgyny reassessed by open-ended self-descriptions'. *Social Psychology Quarterly,* **56**, pp. 278–287.
Walker, A. (1970) *Stardom: The Hollywood Phenomenon.* New York: Stein and Day.
Westin, A. (1970) *Privacy and Freedom.* New York: Atheneum.
Williams, T. M. (1985) 'Implications of a natural experiment in the developed world for research on television in the developing world'. *Journal of Cross Cultural Psychology,* **16**, pp. 263–87.
Winnicott, D. W. (1965) *The Maturational Processes and the Facilitating Environment.* Lara: The Hogarth Press.
Winston, B. (1998) *Media, Technology and Society – A History: From the Telegraph to the Internet.* London: Routledge.
Winstone, R. (ed.) (1996) *The Benn Diaries.* London: Arrow.
Yano, C. (1997) 'Charisma's realm: Fandom in Japan'. *Ethnology,* **36**, pp. 335–49.

Index

Adams, Victoria 'Posh Spice', 99
Adie, Kate, 121, 126
Adler, A., 40, 41
Adler, P., 87
Adler, P.A., 87
Albarn, Damon, 35, 38, 104
Alexander the Great, 14–15, 34, 45, 129
Ashmore, R.D., 77
Augustus, 15

Barnum, P.T., 20–1, 30
Beckham, David, 99, 123, 124, 125
Benn, Tony, 26–7
Bentley, Derek, 23
Black, Cilla, 100, 125
Blackburn, Tony, 88
Boorstin, D. 4
Boswell, James, 18, 47, 130
Botham, Ian, 119
Brando, Michael, 86
Braudy, L., 3, 4, 14, 17, 18, 30, 39, 45, 49, 75, 82, 112, 130, 154
Brown, Divine, 121, 124, 125
Brummell, Beau, 18
Byron, Lord, 18, 34, 45, 47

Caesar, Julius, 4, 86
Caligula, 111
Capone, Al, 28
Cave, Nick, 136
celebrity
  autographs, 139
  and bad behaviour, 8–9, 136–7
  commodification 19, 85–8
  definition of, 3–4
  and divinity, 103–4, 136–7
  encounters with fans, 140–2
  idea of 'gift', 34, 45, 84, 104

as 'guardian angels', 137–8
'inappropriate' letters to, 143–4
interviews, 88–9
and multiple selves, 86–8
mythology, 86
and 'private life', 98
relics, 138–9
responsibilities, 104, 107
rudeness, 10, 92
and 'stardom', 114–5
threat from overkill, 150
Chaplin, Charlie, 91, 100
Chapman, Mark, 144
Chatterton, Thomas, 81–2
Chaucer, Geoffrey, 16–17, 48–9
Christie, Linford, 113, 121, 125
Cicero, 15, 41, 42, 95, 111
Clifford, Max, 116
Clinton, Bill, 121, 124
Clough, Brian, 136
Cobain, Kurt, 83–4, 104
Comstock, G., 56
Condry, J., 57
Cooper, Alice, 86
coyote, severed head sent to celebrity, 143
Csikszentmihalyi, M., 57
Cohen, J., 64
Cross, S.E., 76, 77
cyberspace, 149, 150, 151

Dante Alighieri, 16
Danziger, K., 73
Davis, Bette, 61
Dexys Midnight Runners, 79–80
Dyer, R., 84

Edwards, Eddie 'the Eagle', 25, 101, 115, 125

INDEX

Edwards, Richey, 84-5
Elizabeth I, 49, 50
Erasmus, 17
Erikson, E., 44
Eubank, Chris, 9, 87, 103
Evans, Chris, 121, 125

fame
  accidental, 115-16, 126
  amorality of, 17, 27
  by association, 116, 134
  and 'career landmarks', 120
  definition of, 3, 109
  domain-specific, 5-6, 117
  explanations for, 100-1
  and 'greatness', 36, 39, 112
  international fame, 118-19
  localised fame, 5, 111-12, 117
  and loneliness, 95
  loss of, 81-2
  meritocratic, 111, 112-14
  national fame, 118
  for originality, 114
  preparedness for, 107-8, 126, 156
  as process, 4-5
  and privacy, 96-9
  and relationships, 93-5, 99
  as self-fulfilling prophecy, 38
  and 'self-handicapping', 82
  trajectories of, 119-20
  as vulgar, 33-4
  unwanted, 29-30, 33
fandom, 129-45
  encounters with celebrities, 140-2
  etymology, 130
  fan clubs, 129, 131-2
  pathologizing of fans, 131, 135, 137
  religiosity and, 134-9
  reponsibilities to fans, 104
  stalking, 126, 129, 142-5
  'textual poachers', 131-2
Firth, Colin, 65
Flock of Seagulls, A. 119
Florence Lawrence, 21-2
Floyd, Keith, 95
Foucault, M., 10

Franklin, Benjamin, 18, 73
Fraser, Angus, 118
Freud, S., 37, 38, 40, 44
Fry, Stephen, 106
Funk, Freddie, 117, 118, 121

Galton, Francis, 36, 37, 40
Gamson, J., 19, 46, 130, 131, 132
Garbo, Greta, 90
Garratt, S., 133, 134, 143
Gedo, J., 37, 43
Geertz, C., 74, 97
Gergen, K.J., 75, 77, 78, 88
Goss, Luke, 103
Grable, Betty, 61
Grant, Hugh, 99, 121

Hamilton, Thomas, 27
Harré, R., 77
Harris, Rolf, 93, 100
Hayworth, Rita, 61
Healey, Denis, 27, 112
Hemingway, Ernest, 43, 82-3, 86
Henry VIII, 17, 50
Hickley, John Jr., 144-5
Hillsborough, 117
Hoffman, Dustin, 8-9
Holbein, Hans, 17, 116
Hollywood, 4, 19, 21-5, 61, 130, 142
holography, 151
Homer, 3, 14
homosexuality, 37, 41-2, 48-9, 96, 132
Horace, 49
Hurley, Elizabeth, 99

Internet, the, 149, 150, 152, 154

Jack the Ripper, 27
Jackson, Michael, 30-1, 125
Jaynes, J., 13, 14, 38, 138
Jenkins, H., 131, 132, 135, 137
Jesus Christ, 15, 129
Jindra, M., 135
Johnson, Samuel, 130

Keeler, Christine, 116
Kray, Ronnie, 34, 45

Kray Twins, the, 28–9, 36–7, 114
Kubey, R., 57

Leets, L., 63, 143, 144
Lewinsky, Monica, 116
Little Albert, 121
loneliness, 95, 106

McDonald, D.G., 59, 150, 151
McDonald, Jane, 71, 116
McHugh, M.P., 63
Madson, L., 76, 77
Mahapatra, M., 102, 135, 136
Marshall, P.D., 4, 19, 72, 101
Major, James, 99
Major, John, 111, 123, 125
Manic Street Preachers, 84–5
Marr, Johnny, 34
Maslow, A., 73, 75
mass media
  indiscrimate treatment of the famous, 5, 22, 26–7
  'narrowcast' media, 150
  paparazzi, 29, 97, 99, 137
  'public access' media, 67–1, 129
  radio, 23, 55, 62, 128, 150
media 'effects'
  parasocial interaction 54, 59, 60, 61–7, 90, 128, 139, 145, 148, 151, 154, 155
  responses to 'erotica', 65
  responses to horror, 66
  responses to romance, 66
  uses-and-gratifications theory, 62, 128, 148
Mellor, David, 112
Mercury, Freddie, 84
Metzger, M., 64
Milardo, R., 93
Milton, John, 37
Morrissey, Steven, 34–6, 38, 45, 79, 104
Much, N., 102, 135, 136

Napoleon Bonaparte, 18
Nass, C., 59, 60
Neuman, W.R., 148
Nirvana, 83–4
Nolan, Paul, 25–6, 115, 154

Numan, Gary, 106–7, 142

Oasis, 8, 114
O'Connor, Sinead, 85
O'Donnell, Robert, 82

Palin, Michael, 118
Persaud, Raj, 121
Petrarch, 50, 90, 129
photography, 50–1
Picasso, Pablo, 82–3
pop stars
  as interviewees, 6–7
  pop lyrics, 78–80
  pampered by record companies, 7–8
  'selling out', 80–1
  and sincerity, 84
  taken seriously, 78–9
pork butchery, fame for, 117, 118
postmodernism, 51
Prince Charles, 123, 125, 141
Princess Diana, 97, 125, 126
privacy
  cross-cultural factors, 97–8
  intrusion, 96, 99, 126
  loss of personal space, 94–5
  'private life', 98
  and the private bedroom, 74, 98

Queen, The, 70, 93, 123, 124, 125, 126

Rachmaninov, Sergei, 43
razor, disposable, sent to celebrity, 143
reality
  hyperreality, 51
  representational, 59–60
Reece, Maureen, 4, 25, 33–4, 69–70, 115, 119, 121, 123, 125, 154
Reeves, B., 59, 60
relationships
  parasocial, 59–67
  size of networks, 92, 96
religion
  Christianity and the Western self, 74–5
  concept of the afterlife, 49

INDEX

divinity constructed by Kalasis, 102–3, 135–6
  and fandom, 134–9
  influence of Christian church, 49, 50
  relics, 138–9
Ridley, Emma, 26
Rome, Ancient, 15, 75–6, 111, 112
Rousseau, Jean-Jacques, 18, 35–6, 38, 47, 95, 130
Rowland, Kevin, 79–80
Rubin, R.C., 63
Russell, Bertrand, 41
Ryan, Michael, 27

St Augustine, 15
sausages, route to fame, 117
Scannell, P., 62
Schaller, M., 79
schizophrenia, 37, 42
Schumann, Robert, 42
Seles, Monica, 95, 145
self, the
  cross-cultural factors, 74
  and divine possession, 102
  'gloried' self, 87
  and identity, 77
  individualism, 72–5, 149
  insincerity, 82–5, 141–2
  multiplicity of, 77, 86–8, 95, 151
  and the pop lyric, 78–80
  self-construal, 76–7
  and 'true' self, 77, 78–85, 88, 92
Shakespeare, William, 113
Shapiro, M.A., 59, 150, 151
Shatner, William, 131
Sherif, M., 114
Simonton, D.K., 36, 37, 38, 39, 40, 41, 43, 82, 120
sociobiology, 46–7, 48
Star Trek
  actor as victim of stalking, 132
  Captain Kirk, 131
  erotic encounters between Kirk and Spock, 132
  parallels with the Gospels, 135
  the 'temple of Trek', 135
  'Trekkies', 131–2, 135, 140
Starr, Freddie, 87–8
Straw, Jack, 121
submarine, toy, sent to celebrity, 143
suicide, 81–5

television
  and children, 57, 58–60
  cross-cultural studies of, 57
  digitization, 149
  'fly-on-the-wall' documentaries, 69–71
  future of, 148–54
  psychology of, 55–6
  rise in popularity, 24
  as symbolic replicator, 51–2
  'talk' shows, 68–9
  tele-literacy, 59–60
Turkle, S., 151

Van Gogh, Vincent, 42
Vedder, Eddie, 103–4, 105
Virgil, 4, 16, 49
virtual reality, 150–1
Viz comic, 141
Vonk, R., 77

Weaver, Sigourney, 105–6
Weller, Paul, 79
Williams, Kenneth, 96, 106
Williams, Rachel, 35
Williams, Robbie, 96–7
Winfrey, Ophra, 101
Winston, B., 152
Woodward, Louise, 29–30, 33, 123, 125
Wordsworth, William, 81